on

ager

Superstar
Leadership

SUPERSTAR LEADERSHIP

A 31-DAY PLAN TO MOTIVATE PEOPLE, COMMUNICATE POSITIVELY, AND GET EVERYONE ON YOUR SIDE

RICK CONLOW AND DOUG WATSABAUGH

CAREER
PRESS
Pompton Plains, NJ

SUPERSTAR LEADERSHIP
EDITED BY JODI BRANDON
TYPESET BY EILEEN MUNSON
Printed in the U.S.A.

To order this title, please call toll-free 1-800-CAREER-1 (NJ and Canada: 201-848-0310) to order using VISA or MasterCard, or for further information on books from Career Press.

The Career Press, Inc.
220 West Parkway, Unit 12
Pompton Plains, NJ 07444
www.careerpress.com

Library of Congress Cataloging-in-Publication Data
Conlow, Rick.
  Superstar leadership : a 31-day plan to motivate people, communicate positively, and get everyone on your side / by Rick Conlow and Doug Watsabaugh.
     pages cm
  Includes bibliographical references and index.
  ISBN 978-1-60163-265-4 -- ISBN 978-1-60163-528-0 (ebook) 1. Supervision of employees. 2. Personnel management. 3. Leadership. I. Watsabaugh, Doug, 1951- II. Title.
  HF5549.12.C667 2013
  658.4'092--dc23
                    2012049266

We dedicate this book to
our families who support us,
all the great managers
we have worked with over the years
who have become students of the game,
and all managers
who are fighting the good fight
by doing business
with integrity and a caring attitude.

THE AGENDA

INTRODUCTION

Although CEOs can be worth millions to their companies, their strategies and tactics are often of little practical use to the manager in a manufacturing plant, technology department, restaurant, hospital, or car dealership. *Superstar Leadership* fills in that gap.

Most leadership books today focus on what the CEOs or executives of big companies do. Business executives are real hot stuff. In a company of 32,000 employees or 200 employees, there is only one president. What about the rest of the managers? What do they do of value? Can we learn from them? What practical advice or strategies will help them do a better job? Too often, everyone gets excited about the success of a CEO at a Fortune 500 company because he increased the value of the company's stock and retired and wrote a book. Now, he's on the speaking tour.

CEOs aren't the best to learn from, anyway, because they live in a different world than other managers. For the most part, they are insulated from their customers and employees. Besides, we have seen too many of them cater to the analysts on Wall Street, become involved in shady business practices, and end up on the front-page news in a scandal or in a federal court being prosecuted. Too many underperform and are overpaid. Their driving motivations are greed, self-aggrandizement, ego fulfillment, political connections, and their pocketbooks. They can destroy a company, like what happened at Enron. Of course, these are examples of the bad bosses. To be fair, there are many good CEOs.

This isn't a book that summarizes years of statistical research or surveys results. You will see references to industry research throughout the book to support the Leadership strategies. The practices within *Superstar Leadership* are based on 40 combined years of management experience in addition to our 15 years together spent as business consultants. WCW Partners is our performance-improvement consulting business that has mentored managers from a variety of businesses worldwide to achieve record-breaking performance. The advice you find within these pages isn't based on surveys or anecdotes. It is based on sound research and time-proven strategies that we have seen work again and again.

Superstar Leadership is a personal leadership guide and "workshop" in one, aimed at supervisors and managers who don't always have the resources available to top executives but collectively make a greater impact on their organization's bottom line. It is written for the non-CEO manager, although many CEOs could benefit from it. However, you don't have to be the CEO or on the cover of *Time* magazine to be a Superstar leader.

The Superstar Leadership Model provides a developmental process that helps managers take a critical look at their management approach and competencies, build on strengths, shore up weak areas, and become more effective bosses immediately.

There are nine interrelated strategies and corresponding competencies that have proven successful in a variety of companies and are ripe with real-life examples from our years of experience as leadership consultants inside and outside organizations. After adopting the Superstar Leadership strategies, an 80-year-old company in Canada improved sales to existing customers 75 percent in just one year. Another business put the concepts to work to achieve 20- to 30-percent improvement a year, every year, over five years.

Someone once said, "If you want your people to be better, you have to be better." And though this book speaks to managers, it is employee-centered, with two defining questions:

1. What do employees need from you, the boss, to succeed?
2. What is it like to be supervised by you?

Too many managers have read books and attended seminars, only to shelve the book and binder, and continue to do the same things. In this day and age, with the information and research available, it's inexcusable to be a bad or mediocre boss.

Superstar Leadership strategies are adaptable to every personality and work style, and will fit perfectly to help managers who tackle today's toughest problems. These include bigger goals, absenteeism, turnover, labor shortages, budget cuts, expense controls, distribution shortages, quality problems, improving competition, worldwide competition, government interference, price pressures, strikes, and continuously new technological applications. And they have no time to waste.

Here are four ways to use *Superstar Leadership*:

1. After reading the Introduction, circle the topic areas of most interest and read them. We recommend you also read Day 1, Day 2, and Day 3, for they lay a foundation behind all the topics. Also, make sure you read Day 29 and Day 30, which cover execution. Knowledge is not power; applied knowledge is power.

2. Read the book at your leisure as you would any book you read and apply the applications at work.

3. Use the book as a structured, 31-day improvement plan. Read one topic a day and act on the material each day. Within that time period, you can literally revolutionize the performance of your work team.

4. Use the book as a resource when you are confronted with challenges on the job. We have written the book so the skills are broken down into bite-size pieces that you can always reference when you need to.

In all cases, apply what you learn, and use it to become a better boss or even a Superstar Leader. The differences are daily consistency and passion. You will reap the benefits of positive improvements in your behavior and attitudes. Your employees will achieve increased performance because of your changes and example. Employees and colleagues will notice the difference in your approach and demeanor. Your company will experience the superior results.

So why not dig in? The call for effective leadership is ever-present. People can achieve incredible results with better leaders modeling the way. If you're serious about becoming a better boss, get started with the Warm-Up Activity on page 13, and may the best of success be yours!

WARM-UP ACTIVITY

DIRECTIONS: Before you begin reading and working with the material, consider these questions and write your responses. Doing so will help you focus on what you want to accomplish. Then review the goals and the 31-day agenda for this book.

Name:
Years of supervisory/management experience:
Present job title:
Career goal:
How do you feel about your career success so far?
What are you most proud of?
What are you biggest challenges?
Most rewarding aspect of being a manager or supervisor:
Most frustrating aspect of being a manager or supervisor:
Leadership strengths (what I do well):
Learning expectations (what I need to do better):

SUPERSTAR LEADERSHIP GOALS

1. Define nine leadership strategies of a superstar leader.

2. Assess your strengths and areas for improvement as a leader.

3. Apply the nine strategies to help yourself and your employees achieve and sustain high performance if not superstar results.

SUPERSTAR LEADERSHIP SKILLS: INTRODUCTION

DAY 1: Superstar Leadership Skills Test

DAY 2: What Motivates People, Really?

DAY 3: The High-Performance Formula

Day 1
SUPERSTAR LEADERSHIP
SKILLS TEST

Think of the worst supervisor or boss you ever had. Chances are some-one comes immediately to mind. Why do you consider this person "the worst"? How did he or she act? How did this bad boss's approach affect your attitude and work effort? Did this person influence you to do your best? Jot down your responses under the "Worst Boss" column on page 18.

Now, think of a situation where you had the best boss ever. (It's harder to identify a boss who shines, isn't it?) What was this person like, and what did he or she do differently? How did this person affect you and your work effort? Write in your responses under the "Best Boss" column on page 18.

Did you want to do a better job for the best boss versus worst boss? Of course!

Regrettably, it's far more likely that the majority of our work life has been spent reporting to bad bosses. Bad bosses continue to dominate the landscape of corporate America today. Despite the research on effective leadership and companies' profit and loss statements, bad bosses are an epidemic killing off employee productivity and creativity and company profit potential.

It's a gloomy picture if we feel we can't alter it. But we can.

Knowing how dismal it can be to work for a bad boss, we can decide to be the good boss. And if we have a few rough edges (and don't we all?), we can get them polished. Maybe you can become a Superstar leader.

We know what you're thinking: What about those awful bosses who get great results? Yes, it does seem that some businesses progress in spite of the pitiful practices of managers and supervisors. In fact, if you talk to enough people, you'll find poor bosses and Superstar leaders can both achieve organizational objectives. The difference is in the how and in what happens long term. Lack of respect and poor relationships are weak fuel, leaving poor bosses with nothing to drive sustainable results. Results are unsustainable because poor bosses sap employees' commitment and posi-tive emotion to invest their best in their work.

Worst Boss	Best Boss

In other words, bad bosses' behavior does eventually catch up with them (or their organizations), but, unfortunately for their victims, it doesn't seem to happen fast enough.

So how do you know whether you're a "worst" boss or a "best" boss?

Look at your results. The number-one reason employees say they quit is because of unhappiness with their boss. Employees with bad bosses are four times more likely to leave than employees who believe they have Superstar leaders. Interviews in 700 companies of two million employees suggest that the productivity of employees depends on their relationship to their boss.[1]

The worst bosses contribute to poor morale and bad attitudes, which lead to poor productivity, indifferent customer service, lower sales, reduced quality, and poorer overall financial results. They have employee turnover problems and often have to coerce or bribe employees to do things. Employees perform because they have to, not because they want to. They are like mercenary soldiers being paid to do the job. They aren't the spirited patriots fighting to protect their homes.

In big companies, poor bosses stand on every step of the corporate ladder. In smaller organizations, the owners or key executives are often the culprits. In fact, evidence suggests that there are many bad bosses out there:

▸ Eighty percent of employees say they get no respect at work.[2]

▸ Less than 55 percent of Americans are satisfied with their jobs, compared with 61.1 percent 20 years ago.[3]

▸ Fifty-four percent of employees in lower-performing companies are disengaged.[4]

▸ Companies with higher morale have 16-percent greater share price than companies with lower morale.[5]

We have categorized the bad bosses. We bet you'll recognize some of these examples:

The Dictator: The president of a food company habitually yelled and swore at people to get them to do things. He bullied people into doing what he wanted. It was "his way or the highway," as the saying goes. Not surprisingly, he had huge employee turnover issues, and he was fired within two years.

The Criticizer: An operations manager at a computer-consulting company typically interrupted her managers' meetings many times to criticize their decision-making in front of their employees while rapping her bracelets on the conference table. Morale was poor and creativity low. The place was in a constant state of chaos.

The Liar: A sales executive routinely lied to other department managers about customer issues and, of course, denied it. He often wondered out loud about the lack of teamwork in the company. Departments were always at each others' throats.

The Harasser: In a medical clinic, the general manager flirted openly with and groped female employees with impunity. Employee attitudes were poor, and turnover was high.

The Bully: In the car industry, a manager led with the philosophy "Keep whipping them until the blood runs dry." He constantly browbeat people and put them at odds with one another.

The Micromanager: This manager couldn't delegate; she had her hands in everything. The employees resented it and felt they were being treated like children. Poor attitudes prevailed.

Mr. Nice Guy: In another company, the manager was a good listener and nice person, but he didn't make decisions. Problems festered and weren't resolved. Results were mediocre. He was liked, but few people respected him.

Think about it: Would you wake up in the morning and get all excited about giving it your all for one of these bosses? What's the matter with these supervisors or managers, anyway? Haven't they ever attended a management seminar or read a leadership book? And what's wrong with their bosses? You'd think all of them would know better. These practices don't motivate people.

Why do they do this? For some, it's the opportunity to flex their position power. Others are imitators—just mimicking what was done to them. And yet others simply have poor people skills. Some are just lazy and don't care. On average, 50 percent of managers fail in their positions. An analysis of 12 studies indicates that managers fail 30–67 percent of the time.[6] They most often fail because of personality or relationship issues:

▶ Bad judgment.

▶ Inability to lead teams.

▶ Problems in relationships.

▶ Inability to manage themselves.

▶ Inability to learn from their mistakes.

Additionally, management failure is often linked to poor communications skills that result in diminishing the impact of their other strengths.[7]

The few truly Superstar leaders are refreshingly different and give us all hope that we can help our employees and companies succeed by bringing out the best in people. Superstar leaders create a positive environment for employees so they want to do their best and achieve the highest standards. Their working relationships with employees are positive and respectful. Their organization's business results are consistently good and often outstanding.

Grocery store management and union employees along the West Coast were recently at odds over their new contract. Employees voted to strike—except for one grocery store chain. One hundred percent of the union employees voted against the strike and stayed on the job. Amid industry difficulties, the chain thrived, and the owner shared bonuses with all the employees from bountiful profits.

This is the most exciting time ever to be a leader in an organization. The work of Blanchard, Hersey, Drucker, Goleman, Bennis, Covey, Kouzes and Posner, Reicheld, and others has given managers and supervisors a blueprint that clearly identifies the qualities and behaviors of better bosses, at least at the executive level.[8] If you're a leader who isn't familiar with the work of these individuals or others like them, it's like flying a plane without being trained. You're fiddling with the instruments and controls indiscriminately. Either you won't get off the ground or you'll crash.

If you're familiar with only some of these management gurus, you have learning to do. Being a good boss isn't an event; you have to be a student of the game and commit to lifelong learning. You seldom make money in the stock market through a single or random investment. The rewards come from a sound investment strategy implemented through time. In this book, start executing the strategies immediately as you learn about them. Work at it daily, do the applications, be persistent, stay positive, and you will be recognized as one of the best, if not a Superstar.

In *Superstar Leadership*, we synthesize all of this management thought and mix in practical experience to give you tools and ideas you can apply now at every level of leadership, including the president or CEO.

Throughout the years, we have gathered the following statistics about managers. We asked three questions and noticed the results on the next few pages:

1. How effective is management today?
2. How does this affect employee satisfaction and engagement?
3. What do leaders need to do to create a positive work environment and high performance?

How Effective Is Management Today?

▶ Fifty percent of managers fail in their jobs. An analysis of 12 studies found the failure rate at 30–67 percent.[9]

▶ Fifty percent of managers didn't know improving service/quality would reduce operating cost.[10]

▶ Fifty percent of managers didn't understand that people repeat behavior that is rewarded.[11]

▶ Sixty percent of managers didn't think it is right to brag about an employee in front of others.[12]

▶ Two-thirds of managers don't set goals with their employees.[13]

▶ Seventy percent of managers didn't believe the best way to solve an employee problem is through a mutual decision-making process.[14]

▶ Eighty percent of managers don't know that observations in performance feedback should focus on specifics, not generalities.[15]

▶ Eighty to 95 percent of service/quality problems are management-related.[16]

▶ Ninety-one percent of employees want and would like more recognition, and only 50 percent say they get any at all.[17]

Based on these percentages, how would you grade these managers: A, B, C, D, or F?

If you recognize these behaviors as those of bad bosses, you'll probably give them failing grades. There is no good reason to be a bad boss; the resources to become better managers are available and easy to access. Managers of today have to be better than this!

Now, how does all of this affect employees today?

How Does This Affect Employee Satisfaction and Engagement?

▸ Fifty percent of employees say that their managers fail to make them feel valued and important.[18]

▸ Fifty percent of employee time is idle and they do no work.[19]

▸ Fifty-five percent of employees are unsatisfied with their jobs.[20]

▸ Sixty-five percent of employees say they weren't recognized at all last year.[21]

▸ Seventy to 80 percent of the workforce are disengaged and not committed to the company's goals.[22]

▸ Eighty percent of employees say they get no respect at work.[23]

▸ Eighty-one percent of employees are considering leaving their jobs when economic conditions get better.[24]

▸ Eighty-eight percent of employees feel that there is not enough acknowledgment of their work.[25]

How effective are employees if this is how they are feeling? They certainly aren't going the extra mile. They are doing just enough to get by. Are they as productive as they can be? No. As we have described and shown, people can and want to do a better job. The key is the manager. The manager's attitude and behavior supersede the organization. The working climate the manager creates and his or her people skills in dealing with his or her team will determine the success or failure the manager achieves.

So we asked the next question and learned what Superstar leaders do as we worked with many in various companies.

What Do Leaders Need to Do?

▸ Clear goals and expectations: 16-percent improvement.[26]

▸ Training: Companies in top quarter of training expense ($1,500 per year or more) average 24-percent higher profit margins.[27]

▸ Communication: 30-percent increase in market value.[28]

▸ Coaching: 88-percent impact.[29]

▸ Leadership flexibility: 15–20 percent more results.[30]

▸ Recognition: Triple return on equity for companies with more recognition than those companies that do less.[31]

▸ Promotions/incentives: 22-percent impact on results.[32]

▸ Customer loyalty: 5-percent improvement in customer retention improves profit 25 percent or more![33]

▸ Hiring, personnel policy service: the right way to hire saves three times the annual salary of an employee.[34]

Our experience helping company leaders achieve dramatic business improvements and this research led us to create the Superstar Leadership Model, as shown here. It illustrates the nine strategies of Superstar leaders. This book will do a deep dive into each of these areas, and give you the opportunity to practice and apply them.

Superstar Leadership Model
How to Revolutionize Performance

As we write, we just finished working with a company in the Boston area. We met with the employees, and the camaraderie was awesome. They were joking, sharing ideas, communicating, and involved. In a little more than a year, a new manager had helped them improve their performance significantly across the board. A union steward actually attended the meeting on an off day and afterward thanked the manager!

If we took your employees and others you work with aside and asked, "Is [*boss's name*] a good boss or bad boss?" what would they say? How would you rate, really?

It's true that on any given day, an employee might say his or her manager is poor because of differences of opinion or a decision the employee didn't like. But we're talking about a consistent pattern of behavior and character—as well as results—that define you in the eyes of your employees and those you work with. If you want to improve your effectiveness and care about the people you work with, and if you're willing to change, conduct an honest self-evaluation using the Superstar Leadership Skills Test on pages 24 as a starting point. It consolidates what we've learned from thousands of employees and managers we've worked with throughout the last 30 years. Take a few minutes and rate yourself.

Good boss or bad boss, which one are you? Will you become a better boss? Will you become a Superstar leader? This book is dedicated to helping you achieve a dramatic positive effect on the people you work with and then, more importantly, helping you achieve extraordinary results with them.

Superstar Leadership Skills Test

Directions: Check those areas that apply to you. How do you rate? How would your employees rate you? (Look for a more detailed assessment on line at *www.wcwpartners.com.* Click Superstar Leadership Assessment. It's free.)

Best Boss	Worst Boss
☐ Sets clear expectations with definitive goals and plans	☐ Has unclear or inconsistent objectives/standards
☐ Communicates positively and proactively	☐ Communicates poorly and negatively
☐ Coaches effectively and consistently	☐ Lacks good coaching skills
☐ Recognizes and rewards good performance	☐ Gives primarily negative performance feedback
☐ Provides training and ongoing learning opportunities	☐ Provides little training or learning opportunities
☐ Leads with flexibility, creativity, and integrity	☐ Leads ineffectively, inconsistently, and dishonestly
☐ Creates promotions, incentives, and fun at work	☐ Establishes a routine, status quo work culture
☐ Focuses on continuous improvement in quality and customer service	☐ Talks about service and quality but makes minimal progress
☐ Hires effectively	☐ Experiences high turnover with slipshod hiring practices
☐ Overall, creates a positive, constructive, and team-oriented work environment. The job gets done in exemplary style. Productivity, quality, and service are high, and employee turnover is low.	☐ Overall, establishes a negative and antagonistic work environment. Work gets done; good results are unsustainable. Poor results prevail. Ill feelings and a revolving door ensue.

Superstar Leader Application

You can learn to be a better boss—even a Superstar leader—through ongoing training, coaching, and application. It won't necessarily be easy, and it will require personal change. If you want your people to aspire to high performance, you have to make that your goal, too. It is truly the signature of a Superstar leader to execute the approaches described in this book, in his or her own style, and succeed at them.

If you want to improve your effectiveness, care about the people you work with; and if you are willing to change, use this book as a starting point for an honest self-evaluation and growth program. Participate fully by completing each daily application. You will learn and apply practical and proven leadership practices that will help you and the people you supervise improve performance dramatically and more quickly. We have no doubt that after you read the material and do the leadership activities in this book, you will be well prepared and positioned to inspire the people you work with to achieve outstanding performance.

Notice the graphic that follows this paragraph, the WCW Change Model. It identifies six areas that we have learned from personal experience and success that accelerate positive change in people. Those areas defined are:

- ▶ **Perception**—Self-reflection on your personal strengths/ weaknesses and your view of the world.

- ▶ **Plan**—Establishing a sense of direction, destination, and the goals/actions steps to support it.

- ▶ **Preparation**—Acquiring the skills and knowledge to enhance your ability to improve and adjust your approach to your career or life.

- ▶ **Practice**—Building conviction by applying new skills/ knowledge through consistent simulation, application, repetition, and review of results.

- ▶ **Persistence**—Continuing determined efforts and establishing robust confidence in spite of fears, obstacles, and challenges embodied in change.

- ▶ **People**—Surrounding yourself with people who are supportive to help you stay the course and provide you with insight to help ramp up results.

We have built our applications and action planning at the end of this book around these concepts to give you the best opportunity to improve your leadership effectiveness. (We also have an individual study program which includes a leadership assessment, a *Superstar Leadership* workbook, and three DVDs that give you further exercises and tools to become a Superstar leader. Check out: *wcwpublishing.com/#* for this resource.)

WCW Partners Change Model

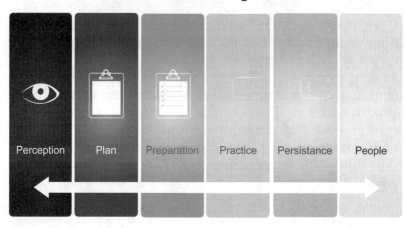

| Perception | Plan | Preparation | Practice | Persistence | People |

Day 1 Superstar Leader Application
What did you learn about yourself as a leader after taking the Superstar Leadership Skills Test?
What do your employees need from you to excel?
What is it like to work for you?
What is one thing you already do that you need to keep doing?
What is one thing you can improve upon today?

We are what we repeatedly do; excellence is not an act but a habit.

—Aristotle

Day 2
WHAT MOTIVATES PEOPLE, REALLY?

When we work with managers across the country, the most often asked question is: "How do you motivate people?" It's as if there is a magic wand to wave or a pill they can take to inspire those who seem to lack motivation. The truth is that everyone is already motivated. It's just that many employees aren't passionate about or committed to the things managers want them to do or accomplish. Sure, the employees have a job and want to do it well enough to get paid and not get fired, but what is it that will motivate them to want to do better, keep learning, and go the extra mile?

In his classic article, "One More Time: How Do You Motivate Employees?" Frederick Herzberg seems irritated by managers' continued concern about motivation. Maybe we just need to pay attention. According to his work, the factors that motivate most people are:[1]

- Achievement.
- Advancement.
- Recognition.
- Growth.
- The work itself.
- Learning.
- Responsibility.

Our opportunity as managers is to leverage these factors to enrich employees' jobs.

Notice that money isn't on the list. The reason is that just as many people say money is a job dis-satisfier as it is a job satisfier. Plus, Herzberg argues that incentives are more of kick in the pants than a motivator. A kick in the pants can be negative or positive, fear-based, or monetary incentive–based. Herzberg says both produce movement, not motivation. Movement means there is a change in results, but largely because the manager took action rather than the employee. This lacks sustainability. Motivation means the employee has an internal generator to want to do the job better or more effectively, and isn't influenced by an external reward or carrot. This produces more consistent efforts.

Many studies support this and find direct links to creating stellar employee engagement and motivation and bottom-line business results. For example, *Fortune Magazine*'s "100 Best Companies to Work for in America" consistently outperform the market and competition. The

Corporate Leadership Council summarizes many of these research reports. The evidence continues to grow to show a direct link between employee retention, customer retention, and profitability.[2] Recently, Alex Edmans at the University of Pennsylvania, The Wharton School, summarized his research in the paper "Does the Stock Market Fully Value Intangibles? Employee Satisfaction and Equity Prices?" He analyzed the relationship between employee satisfaction and long-run stock returns. He found *Fortune*'s best companies exhibited significantly more positive results and that employee satisfaction is positively correlated to this.[3] Unfortunately, it seems too few investors and managers alike tend not to value this.

We have asked managers what motivates employees. What do you think was at the top of the managers' list? Money. Why the difference? All too often, managers don't understand motivation or engagement, and don't give employees want they want or need in a job. Consequently, employees lack motivation. Poor bosses think that way. Superstar leaders don't.

So how do you motivate people? You don't! You let them motivate themselves. In fact, you find ways to inspire them. The truth is that employees are always motivated. And different things motivate different individuals. Most of the time, managers don't know what is important to an employee.

A manager for a client of ours had a customer service employee who was performing lower than the stated goals. After further study, we learned the employee was newly married, had two small daughters, and lived with his father-in-law. He constantly talked about the need to save money. The manager didn't know this. In discussing the situation with the employee, we learned that he wanted to get his own place for his family. He needed another $500 a month to do it. With coaching and goal-setting sessions, the employee was shown how he could make the money he needed by selling to and servicing his customers. He became a better performer for the company and accomplished his goal to rent his own home.

How do you motivate people? You find out what's important to them and work to design or create an environment that helps them achieve their goals or needs for the company's reasons and their reasons. Although you may not always be able to provide added incentives, with a little creativity, you can structure any job to help an employee win.

Superstar leaders provide three key ingredients that produce the right circumstances for employees to perform at their highest levels: competence, commitment, and climate. These help fulfill the job enrichment described by Herzberg.

By learning and applying these high-performance ingredients in the workplace, you will help your employees:

▸ Accomplish company goals for their reasons.

▸ Provide better quality of work.

▸ Go the extra mile.

▸ Find creative ways to do a better job.

▸ Provide consistent and superior levels of service to customers.

▸ Cooperate with others to do the job better.

▸ Improve their productivity and results.

Poor bosses are oblivious to these motivational principles. Their approach is to yell, scream, threaten, reprimand, abdicate, and even plead.

We have heard employees say, "You can't find a manager when you need one, so what are they for?" Precisely. Leader's who don't engage their people in positive ways find that the employees don't engage their jobs or customers in positive ways; those who do engage reap powerful benefits.

The first step is to look at your work environment and ask yourself these questions about your team:

1. Do the employees want to come to work, or is it a drag?

2. Do they know what's expected of them?

3. Are they well trained to do the job?

4. What do they do well? What can they improve?

5. Are your versions of the above similar to theirs? What are the differences? Have you discussed this with them?

6. Do the employees feel appreciated and rewarded for their efforts?

7. How well do they work as a team?

8. How effective is their customer service or quality of work?

9. Do they routinely go the extra mile?

10. What are the career aspirations of each of your employees? What is one personal goal important to each of them?

11. What's it like working for you? Or how would they rate you as a manager?

12. Are results above average or exceptional? Is progress being made and sustained?

Use your answers to these questions for your Day 2 Superstar Leader Application. In Day 3, we will look at the details of what we call the "High-Performance Formula."

Day 2 Superstar Leader Application
What did you learn from this discussion on motivation?
What do your answers to the 12 questions tell you about how you influence people's motivation?
What steps can you take to more effectively motivate people?

The great secret of success in life is for a man to be ready when his opportunity comes.

—Benjamin Disraeli

Day 3
THE HIGH-PERFORMANCE FORMULA

Here's a simple acronym for creating a high-performance environment where employees want to do a good job and routinely go the extra mile.

High-Performance Formula

$$HP = E^c \times (C+C+C)$$

High Performance = Clear Expectations × (Competence + Commitment + [supportive] Climate)

High Performance

This means reaching and exceeding company goals. It also means finding ways to become consistently better. Eventually, it turns into setting new company standards for results and redefining what is really possible. Superstar leaders inspire people to achieve high performance and to sustain it. Superstar leaders create a climate where employees want to excel in their jobs. It's a function of paying attention to employees' competence, commitment, and the climate of the business or department. Bad bosses don't know how to inspire people or don't really care about learning how to do it. They may talk about it, but it never gets done, so performance results are inconsistent and average at best.

Clear Expectations

All good performance starts with clear expectations and goals. This is all about what are we doing. How are we going to do it together? And why? If people know what results they are accountable for, if they know the plan, tools, resources, and support they have to get there, if they know the payoff, an amazing thing happens: They begin to rise to the occasion and perform better.

Competence

Competence means the employee's job skills and knowledge. In any profession, the best performers continually practice and train to get better at their trade. A concert pianist puts in untold hours to play with effortless grace. Disney provides more training to 18- to 20-year-olds than managers of all ages receive in companies all over the world. Whether they are superstars or not, professional baseball players prepare in the winter and during spring training for the regular season and continue to practice before games throughout the year.

To compete today, managers need to educate and train their employees. We agree that companies should hire competent people first, but then you need to keep them learning. It's been said that "world-class" training is the equivalent of 5 percent of your payroll budget. You might not have that kind of budget or a training department, but you don't need to. Practically speaking, you are committing to weekly, monthly, and quarterly training. It's not always teaching people what they don't know; it's also fine-tuning their current skills and refining what they are capable of doing. Every year, *Fortune* publishes a list of the top 100 best companies to work for. These companies consistently provide more training (50–60 hours per year) per employee per year than other companies.

Commitment

Commitment involves employee willingness and desire to do the job. Most people have this to a certain degree because they want a paycheck. It's been said that the number-one reason people go to work is because the alarm went off to get them up. Though that is stretching the truth, it emphasizes a key principle. People go to work for their reasons, and most want to work. They need to make a living and earn money to pay their way. They aren't doing the job for free. The work and the income create the motivation to do the job.

However, that's not enough today. Business is tough and competitive. We need stellar performances. How do you get people to go the extra mile routinely? Managers need highly productive people. How do you get them to come to work because they enjoy it? How do you get them to want to do the job better and better? We began to talk about that in Day 2 (What Motivates People, Really?). Here's a thought: Which employee will perform better—the one you consistently build up? Or beat up?

Bad bosses have one approach to motivation. As you know, the airline industry has faced challenging times. Many blame it on high gas prices and 9/11. Southwest Airlines has prospered in this tough environment anyway. Why? They have cultivated better relationships with employees and customers than their competitors. Southwest people want to come to work, and they are the most productive in the industry.[1]

The other airlines have poorer relationships with employees and customers. One large airline has this unspoken philosophy for employees:

leave your brains at the door. Now there is a motivational approach! Not surprisingly, this airline has been through bankruptcy, and management continually has contentious relationships with employees and the unions. Bad bosses destroy employee commitment and the desire to excel. Employees come to work because they have to get the paycheck and just go through the motions. They can't wait to leave and go home. Many start looking for a better job. Unfortunately, most bad bosses are oblivious to this employee condition.

These are the telltale signs of poor management practices:

▸ High turnover.

▸ Few new ideas from employees.

▸ Not much employee feedback.

▸ More sick days and absences.

▸ Lower productivity.

▸ Employee teamwork issues.

▸ Poorer customer service.

▸ Quality problems.

▸ Difficulty in maintaining good performance on priority company goals.

▸ Numerous union grievances or confrontations.

▸ Inconsistent results.[2]

Bad bosses use the union as a scapegoat. They blame their problems on the union and the contract. Frankly, the unions hammer out tough contracts because they can't trust management to lead fairly, effectively, or efficiently. The U.S. automobile industry is a perfect example. Let's not forget that workers fought to form unions to protect their rights and jobs from intimidating and abusive management practices. Management has no one to blame but their own anemic leadership practices.

Superstar leaders work with the union if there is one in their company. If there isn't a union, good leadership keeps them out. Too many unions breed mediocre performances. That's part of the reason union membership is on the decline. Unions are often confrontational in their approach, too. We have seen many examples in the media where this plays out. Where leadership inspires and motivates employees through a high-powered, positive work environment, the union isn't needed and is frankly outdated for today's business world.

A Canadian company faced a strike in Vancouver. The unions in British Columbia are as demanding as any. Workers did strike, but the strike was short-lived. When employees came back to work, their performance skyrocketed. Why? Management didn't hold any grudges. By using the Superstar strategies, they created a high-powered work environment. Through specific goals and up-front communication, they cleared the air about issues after everyone came back to work. New training was implemented; management became more hands-on to work with customers. Sales promotions and incentives were added. The management team focused on how to service the customer better by becoming better leaders of people. They built people up and didn't beat them up. Motivation to excel and performance reached record levels. Business results became stellar in a few short months.

Climate

This is all about the work environment. Is it supportive or not? Superstar leaders are supportive; bad bosses aren't. Climate involves:

- A positive, not negative, atmosphere.
- Clear goals, not vague visions.
- Listening, not telling.
- Recognition, not criticism.
- Teamwork, not isolationism.
- Defined values, not rhetoric.
- A sense of purpose, not business as usual.
- Fun and having a good time, not boring and routine.
- Innovative, not same old, same old.
- Integrity, not disreputable practices.
- Clear values, not confusion.

In every family, there is always the fun aunt and the strict aunt, or the fun grandma and the crabby grandma (or uncles and grandpas, as the case may be). When, as a child, you went to the strict relative's house, there was always a list of don'ts: Don't go upstairs. Don't eat anywhere but the kitchen. Don't watch television. Don't play too rough. But the fun relative loved whenever you came over and always had games and snacks. What kid wouldn't prefer that over the list of don'ts? And in appreciation of the special attention, you probably were well mannered when you visited the fun relative.

The climate you create in your department or team sets the tone for the work atmosphere and daily employee behavior. Yet each manager creates his or her own environment within his or her department or area of responsibility. A manager in one of our seminars explained the bad boss scenario with this example:

> In my department, the manager comes in every morning, goes straight to his office, and slams the door shut. He only comes out when there is a problem, and then issues commands and yells at somebody. It's the same every day. One day, I stopped the manager before he made it to his office in the morning and said it would be nice if he could talk to us and say hello. He responded by saying he didn't have time for that trivial crap.

To sum up, people are motivated for their own reasons, but managers influence this positively or negatively with their leadership practices. Superstar leaders learn and apply the High-Performance Formula, which translates into specific leadership practices we identified in the Superstar Leadership Skills Test and that we will begin to discuss in greater detail.

High-Performance Formula
$$HP = E^c \times (C+C+C)$$

High Performance = Clear Expectations × (Competence + Commitment + [supportive] Climate)

The High-Performance Formula fosters the distinct and collective management practices of the Superstar Leadership Model. It focuses the manager day in and day out to bring out the best in employees every day and all the time.

Asset and Liability Leadership

Asset/Effective Leadership

- Clear vision, goals, and expectations
- Engaging recognition
- Proactive communication
- World-class training
- Exemplary mentoring/coaching
- Creative and consistent promotion/incentives

Liability/Ineffective Leadership

- Lack of vision, goals, and clear expectations
- Critical or mostly negative feedback
- Absence of proactive communication
- A lack of training, mentoring, and coaching
- Few promotions/incentives

As a result, employees perform better.

Asset and Liability Performance

Asset/Higher Performance	Liability/Lower Performence
• Higher morale	• Lower morale
• Lower employee turnover	• Higher employee turnover
• Courteous to customers	• Discourteous to customers
• Responsive to customer needs or problems	• Unresponsive to customer needs or problems
• Goes the extra mile	• "Goes through the motions"
• Excellent teamwork	• Lack of teamwork
• Superior service	• Average to poor performance

Then the company has better business results.

Income and Expense Results

Income/Superior Service	Expense/Poor Service
• Growth in sales	• Lost sales
• More and larger repeat purchases	• Smaller and fewer repeat purchases
• Recommend/refer others	• Higher number of complaints
• Higher customer satisfaction index (CSI)	• Lower customer satisfaction index (CSI)

Although running a company effectively requires other things of managers, application of the High-Performance Formula through the Superstar Leadership Model is what it takes to build the highest-performing employees. If there is any secret to leadership and management, it's in the consistent, daily application and execution of this formula and the model—and, being willing and open-minded enough to keep learning.

The rest of the book will provide you with the knowledge and needed skills to passionately apply this formula to achieve improvement and sensational results.

Day 3 Superstar Leader Application
What can you learn from the High-Performance Formula?
What are you doing that contributes to a poor work environment?
What can you do today to develop a supercharged, positive work environment so people want to do a better job?

In the long run, men hit only what they aim at. Therefore...they had better aim at something high.

—Henry David Thoreau

SETTING CLEAR GOALS AND EXPECTATIONS

DAY 4: Performance Management

DAY 5: Giving Feedback

DAY 6: Dealing With Performance Problems

Day 4
PERFORMANCE
MANAGEMENT

Pete is the general manager of a West Coast plant for a national company. He has had trouble meeting his revenue and profit numbers for the last year. His district manager has scheduled a meeting with him to discuss action plans for improvement.

Pete's company is in a highly competitive market, and margins are slim. He has been a general manager for eight years and is known as a tough, no-nonsense boss. He has always made money and reached company goals, but he never has achieved stellar results. This year has been particularly difficult. A bigger national competitor has purchased smaller local companies and lowered prices, and he's losing accounts. He has lost some employees due to turnover and has fired some of his managers for lack of results. Most of his salespeople are new, and new sales have been slow in coming.

Pete's been working long hours, and the stress is getting to him. He has wracked his brain with how to improve results quickly. He has already:

▸ Threatened his management team.

▸ Cut expenses to the bone.

▸ Pulled in favors from a few key accounts.

▸ Fired people.

▸ Held service and sales contests.

▸ Demanded his management team work extra hours and delay vacations.

Unfortunately, results haven't improved. He knew his job was on the line, and he wasn't sure what to do next. However, he would have a plan for his boss with time lines and new projections. He just dreaded the meeting. His boss took no excuses, and would rant and rave at him and his team or make him work the weekend again.

Mary is an experienced manager in the retail industry. She needed to improve sales in her 500 stores. She was gaining 1 percent to 3 percent growth while competition was doing 4 percent to 5 percent over the prior year. She had customer service problems, too. So she held a meeting to talk about the virtues of customer service and followed it up with a few hard-hitting e-mails. Whenever she held a staff meeting, she talked about the importance of customer service. However, there was no plan, measurement, training, recognition, or new resources to help. Not surprisingly, six months later, her customer surveys improved little, and sales didn't improve. Everyone was on pins and needles when she held a meeting, called, or visited a store.

These are typical scenarios and challenges managers face today. How would you rate these managers as bosses? What do you think their employees would say about their leadership? They aren't bad people, and some in upper management would say they are good leaders doing the best they can. What do you think their employees say?

All good performance starts with clear goals and expectations. Superstar leaders know that people want to succeed. Goals motivate people to succeed. Earl Nightingale said years ago, "The problem isn't in achieving goals; people will do that. It's getting them to set the goals in the first place."

A hundred-year-old services company in the United States wanted to improve sales to its existing customers. The results were mediocre. The company had tried a variety of incentives and meetings, and nothing worked. By engaging with the Superstar Leadership Strategies, the company began to make progress. Improvement began with a thorough assessment of sales management's skills in attracting and talking to their larger customers. Tracking reports were created around well-designed goals. These goals were shared with all involved. With consistent communication on the numbers and goals, occasional incentives, follow-up coaching, and regular recognition, improvements were gained and sustained.

What changed? Did the employees decide to become better? Did they get fed up and decide to do it themselves? Did they go to management with big goals and a new plan? Certainly not! The management changed, with some help. They refocused their efforts with new goals, tools, and support.

Poor bosses often lack clear goals and plans. One general manager in a retail organization changed goals and direction so often, he disillusioned his employees, performance suffered, and he lost his job. Other managers simply don't worry about goals. They don't know how to set them; no one showed them how. So they show up every day and do the best they can. Little is discussed about goals or progress. Many bosses have goals, but they forget to tell the employees. If the goals aren't reached, the employees get in trouble or are tormented about the lack of results.

Once people are clear on the goals, you create action plans to achieve them. What is it about this that frightens managers? So few really do it well. Research shows goal-setting is the motivational technique that works and performance will improve. Effective goal-planning is a motivational technique that improves performance in the work place.

To set goals and plans, a manager must:

▶ Think about and create a plan for his or her area, department, or company.

▶ Do this regularly with periodic updates, staying one step ahead of the company process.

▶ Identify department or company strengths and areas of improvement.

▶ Identify each direct report's strengths and areas of improvement.

▶ Analyze customer feedback or quality data.

▶ Consider all relevant information: equipment, the economy, competition, resources, and so forth.

▶ Set SMART (specific, measurable, attainable, relevant, and time-bound) goals on company priorities. Improving customer service is not a SMART goal. It's vague. Improving the customer survey results from 69 percent to 75 percent in the next year is a SMART goal.

▶ Regularly communicate results.

▶ Set goals with each employee, and regularly review progress with them.

We recommend that managers include employees in the process. One manager we met in an airport had just accepted a job as plant manager with a new company and was moving from Memphis to Houston. We could tell he was a good boss based on his actions and how he spoke about the value of his employees. After assuming his new role, one of his first steps included involving his team in a planning process. Why do this? People want to be part of something—the team, a cause, a mission. With their contribution, managers not only achieve that but also tap their minds for creative ideas that they don't have. The employees are committed to the plans because they now "own" them.

How to Manage Performance

All good performance begins with clear expectations and goals—keeping employees' daily focus on excelling in their jobs. When employees understand what managers want and expect, they will stay engaged, want to do their jobs well, and find ways to keep improving. They will perform more effectively and be more satisfied with their jobs. Without this important communication, only the very best employees will excel.

The biggest complaint from managers is that all of this takes time. And it does. However, it's an investment in a process that saves you time later and that can dramatically improve productivity. Here are some key considerations:

Setting Expectations

Meet one-on-one, and review the job description and duties in detail with new employees. Answer their questions and have them talk to others doing the job. Set goals for 30 through 90 days. Meet with the employee periodically to clarify any misunderstandings, review progress, and handle problems. Ask for periodic updates on new projects, and continue to check employees' expectations: first day, first week, first month, and monthly.

Goal-Setting

Meet one-on-one and establish clear goals with all employees. Start the day you hire new employees. Put three to five goals in writing, and clarify what's in it for them, relating their performance to personal impact. Schedule a meeting to discuss this at least monthly, but flex with the challenges and follow-up. This is an invaluable communication process that will help employees succeed. Some companies discuss goals daily, but most managers don't do it at all or do it just once a year at a performance review. That isn't enough; jobs are too fast-paced and complex to let things go that long. Superstar leaders make goal-setting, communication, and feedback on results key priorities.

Coaching

Review employees' performance daily, weekly, monthly, or quarterly, depending on the need. Coaching discussions aren't about pay increases or for job evaluation purposes. Follow your company procedures for those. They are usually required every six months or once a year. Talk about recent, specific performance one-on-one, and review specifically how things are going from two perspectives. First, understand the employee's view. Ask these key questions:

- ▸ How's it going?
- ▸ What's working? (A great time for praise and recognition.)
- ▸ What are your problems or challenges?
- ▸ What can you do differently or better?

While you ask the questions, you should thoughtfully listen to their comments and then give appropriate feedback. For example:

▸ Give positive feedback: *"I agree you did a good job on the report. It was specific and well researched."*

▸ Bring up problems: *"Have you noticed the growth in complaints? What's happening there? How are you handling it?"*

▸ Create a plan of action: *"What about providing menu options for the customer? I haven't seen much of that. Can we focus on that?"*

If you are separated by distance, this can be handled with a phone call. E-mail is inappropriate; it's too impersonal, and we will often write what we might not say in person.

A.M.

Say hello to people in the morning. Do informal coaching, talk to employees, pat them on the back, tell a joke, give them a hand if needed, and listen to what's going on. There are times that your duties might prevent you from doing this, but make every effort to make it a regular practice.

P.M.

Every day, at the end of the day, check in with every employee you can. Keep it informal, and ask things like: *How did it go? What progress did you make? Any problems? Anything you need help with? How important is that goal we talked about? Let's make more of an effort. What's the plan tomorrow? Have a great evening!* Always keep it positive!

Goal Board

Track your priority goals on a bulletin board, an intra-company Web-site, or dashboard. This provides immediate recognition for employees and fans the flame of competition and pride in doing the job well.

Staff Meetings

Meet at least weekly and review progress. Include people in other offices through phone conferences or a WebEx. The meeting doesn't have to be long. You want to get updates on priority goals or projects, discuss problems or issues, and communicate any news about your area or company.

E-Mail/Text

Keep people informed. Communicate progress and results to employees regularly. Without information, people tend to think the worst, and the rumor mill grows. This is especially important to employees in remote offices, who are separated by distance from headquarters. Keep your e-mails positive as well.

Phone Calls

Use for the same reasons as e-mail/text, but it's more personal. Managers of one of our client companies call their reps a couple of times a week to encourage or recognize them. This also gives them the opportunity to find out how things are going. In the beginning, most employees asked, "What's the problem?" They were so used to managers only contacting them with issues. (By the way, use the phone to confront performance issues only if there's no way to meet one-on-one. Then focus on the problem, not the person, and identify a plan for improvement.)

Day 4 Superstar Leader Application
What can you learn from the discussion on performance management?
How have you done this in the past?
What positive changes will you make to achieve better results?

To bring out the best in people, you have to be better!

—Rick Conlow

Day 5
GIVING FEEDBACK

What really motivates people? We've reviewed this in detail, but there's a prominent factor we have yet to discuss: feedback. Performance feedback has been called the number-one motivator of people. Why?

Think about a time when someone really praised you for achieving a goal. How did you feel? Energized? Positive? Did you want to do it again?

Think of a time when someone gave you constructive and honest feedback about what you were doing wrong. How did you feel? Disappointed but determined to do better? Did you want to try out a new skill, idea, or method?

Contrast these with a time you did good work and no one noticed, or a time that you didn't do a good job and were railed at.

The term *feedback* was popularized by the space agency. At first, rockets sent into orbit were off course more than they were on course. It took constant radio signals back and forth to mission control to get the rocket to its destination. The feedback was used to stay on course and to reach the objective.

Kirby Puckett was a Minnesota Twins all-star and helped the Twins win two World Series titles. When he first came up to the big leagues, everyone could see he would be a good player, but it was Twins hitting coach Tony Oliva who helped him polish his game.

Puckett always took extra batting practice, and Oliva consistently stood behind the batting cage and gave him feedback on his technique: "Good swing." "Keep the elbow up." The rest is history.

How many employees really get that kind of support and attention in their jobs? Most companies do performance reviews once or twice a year. They are too often a weak attempt to justify paltry cost-of-living adjustments, or an academic exercise of filling out forms required by human resources or the personnel department. The feedback is most often generalized to fit into job rating categories and couched in broad terms like *good job, he has a good or poor attitude,* or *needs improvement.*

For years, the performance review system of one of the largest automobile manufacturers required that its employees get the highest rating to advance in their careers. Managers' ratings were partially based on their employees' ratings. Soon, nearly all managers were receiving the highest ratings. The system's lack of specific feedback created cultural mediocrity, not continuous improvement. All the while, the company was losing market share to competitors and eventually went bankrupt.

Superstar leaders give specific, constructive, and consistent feedback. Bad bosses don't.

Bill was the president of a growing food company in the Midwest. He advanced in his career because of hard work and determination. He learned the food business well; however, he didn't learn how to deal with people as well. He gave feedback to employees, all right, and he gave it often: Why couldn't they do things the way he did? Bill yelled, swore, and screamed when he gave feedback to try to get people to do things the right way. He fancied himself a great motivator. He could get any employee to do what he wanted after a communication session or two. The company's growth rate stalled under his leadership, he turned over his management team often, and he was eventually fired.

So how do you give effective feedback? It begins with the philosophy that people want to do a good job and they have untold reserves of hidden potential waiting to be put to good use. Given the right circumstances, employee performance can be absolutely astonishing. Why do we have to wait for the Olympics or the Super Bowl to witness championship results? Our job as managers is to help employees discover their potential and ignite their desire to use it.

To be helpful, feedback needs to be immediate and positive. You can't wait for a performance review to give it, and you can't give it only when people screw up. If you wait until the performance review, employees won't hear you. They'll be too focused on their raise, and it will be too broad to be useful. If you wait only for problems to arise, you will come across like a lion tamer cracking a whip to get them to go where you want them to go. You can shatter a person's self-confidence this way. We aren't training lions; we are leading people who have emotions.

Here are some guidelines for feedback:

▸ Give praise immediately.
▸ Be sure your intention is to be helpful and honest about the feedback you plan to give.
▸ Do your homework so you have all available information that may be helpful.

- Check to make sure the person is open to feedback. *"Can I give you some feedback on this?"*
- Be immediate but private when giving negative or constructive feedback about poor performance.
- Be specific. *"You have to do a better job"* is too general. *"I want you to improve handling customer complaints by asking a few more questions. For example..."* is more specific and detailed.
- Use "I" statements. Own the feedback. Don't say, "Others said…" or "We think...." (Use a statement similar to the prior example.)
- Check for understanding. *"How does this sound to you?" "Can you summarize your understanding of what you can do?"*
- Pay attention to the person's emotional response, especially when giving negative feedback. *"You seem concerned about this. What questions or comments do you have?"* Offer additional help or follow-up.
- Encourage the person to seek others' feedback, and keep an open mind to learning about other ways to accomplish the task.

Managers frequently don't give enough positive feedback. They give too much negative feedback in harmful ways: blaming, criticizing, yelling, swearing, name-calling, threatening, comparing to others, or belittling. This leaves the employee dejected, angry, and frustrated. On other occasions, because managers don't know how to give feedback, they delay it, or save it and then dump it all at once when they are fed up. This is called "seagull management." A seagull flies in, makes a lot of noise, dumps on everyone, and then leaves. These are the actions of bad bosses. These are not motivational techniques. Employee performance is hurt by these kinds of antics.

With praise, you make people feel even better about their efforts, and they want to do it again. By following the guidelines for giving negative feedback in a constructive way, you help them feel supported in getting better. You respect them enough to take the time to point out the errors in their performance and show them how to improve. You provide a safe but honest opportunity to develop and enhance positive results.

Feedback will be discussed again as we talk about specific methods for recognition and dealing with performance problems. For now, remember that giving feedback is an essential skill in building effective relationships with employees—a powerful tool that you can use to bring out the best in people and achieve outstanding results.

Day 5 Superstar Leadership Application
What can you learn from this section on giving feedback?
What do you do well in this area?
What can you do better?
Think of an employee who needs constructive negative feedback. Considering the feedback guidelines, how can you handle your discussion so that it's positive and motivational?

Where you begin doesn't matter. Your willingness to start is what counts.

—Rhonda Britten

Day 6
DEALING WITH PERFORMANCE PROBLEMS

Most employees think they are performing better than they are, and all employees have the potential to do better. Dealing with performance problems is a key opportunity to motivate people. Most managers are poor at it. Either they ignore the problem until it becomes so evident that they have to do something, or, when they deal with it, they polarize employees with their negativism or by sandwiching the problem between positive comments. This doesn't work because employees receive mixed messages and too often only hear what they want to hear. Don't be a poor boss with this.

Superstar leaders believe in people and that they want to and can do a good job. So in theory, there aren't bad employees, just employees with behavior problems. There are exceptions to this, but the good boss gives everyone an opportunity to improve. Learn the techniques here, and many employees will thank you.

What are the problems you've faced? Check the ones you've handled:

☐ Absenteeism
☐ Lack of teamwork
☐ Tardiness
☐ Poor communication
☐ Poor quality
☐ Lack of follow-through
☐ Sub-par productivity
☐ Stealing

☐ Low sales
☐ Harassment
☐ Poor customer service
☐ Inappropriate use of time
☐ Customer complaints or company resources
☐ Other employee complaints
☐ Other

Following are ways to handle employee performance problems. Circle the ones you practice:

1. Listen to their concern.
2. Empathize.
3. Ignore it.
4. Be specific.

5. Follow up.

6. Summarize.

7. When talking with the employee, make a list of all of the mistakes (not positive feedback) and require changes within a strict regimen and unrealistic time line.

8. Set action plans.

9. Criticize the employee, and raise your voice as you do.

10. Problem-solve together.

11. Observe and attend to their emotional reaction.

12. Bring up problems with other employees, too.

13. Ask the employee to describe the problem and how he or she thinks it can be improved.

14. Talk about the problem, and compliment the person on his or her capability of succeeding.

15. Transfer the employee to another department.

Items 3, 7, 9, 12, and 15 are obviously methods to ignore. Remember: Each problem is different with each employee. Performance problems are always situational. To be more effective with any problem, apply these general guidelines: Be as immediate as possible, be specific, follow up regularly to check on results, and praise progress.

Through the next few pages, we'll direct our attention to three specific methods of addressing performance problems:

1. Redirection.

2. Review With LEAD.

3. Reprimand.

Redirection

Use redirection with anyone inexperienced in a particular task. This could be a new employee needing to learn a new job or a veteran employee taking on a new job duty. Redirection means to show someone how to do a job correctly. As we discussed earlier, you must give employees clear expectations and goals when they begin a new job or task. You or someone else in the company might need to train them on how to do it as well. Redirection involves closely observing their performance of a new task and again giving them on-the-job training on how to do it right. This is largely one-way, positive communication. Here are the steps:

1. **Present:** Show them how one step at a time.
2. **Practice:** Let them try while you observe and help.
3. **Perform:** Let them try on their own.
4. **Evaluate:** Review their results, point out what's right, see if they can see anything wrong, and then go over mistakes constructively by presenting how again.

Mitch is a customer service representative for a company. He loves customers and provides exemplary service. That's what he was initially trained for. The company came out with a new product, and sales to existing customers became a new priority for the job. Mitch didn't want to sell. He didn't see himself as a salesperson. Anthony was Mitch's supervisor. Through informal coaching, weekly training, positive communication, one-on-ones in the field, and recognition, Anthony helped Mitch learn how to sell and want to sell even more. He taught Mitch that selling was exemplary service, too, because he helped customers with other needs. It was a three-year process, and Mitch became a superstar in the company, dramatically improving his results by a multiple of 20. He also made a great commission. Today, Mitch loves selling and servicing accounts because they are the same thing. Many companies would have fired Mitch in the beginning. Anthony saw the potential. As a Superstar leader, he put in the time, and it paid off in exemplary outcomes.

It is important to praise progress and point out mistakes constructively. For example: "Bill, you did step 1 well, correctly, and on time. In step two, do you notice anything that could be better? You are right; you needed to ask the customer for his serial numbers on the product and record it. Let me review the procedure again."

The redirection steps give you a proven process for on-the-job training, which we will talk more about later when we discuss training.

Review With LEAD

Review With LEAD is a two-way communication and mutual problem-solving process designed to find an acceptable solution or action plan to a performance problem or employee issue. LEAD means to listen, explore, attend, and define a solution. It works better for employees with some experience with a task or goal. Why? Because they have some success in the task. By getting them involved in solving the problem, you use their experience plus yours. You also continue their development to improve or solve the problem on their own in the future.

Use the Review With LEAD method to uncover the specifics of employee performance issues or problems, clarify misunderstandings about the issue or the employee's situation, defuse emotions in "sticky" areas, resolve differences that may arise, handle concerns, and maintain open dialogue. Let's look at each part of the LEAD method in detail from your perspective in dealing with the problem.

Listen

Are you really employee-centered when dealing with problems, or are you preoccupied with other concerns? Your goal is to focus on employee needs and objectives—not a quick resolution so you can go to a meeting.

1. Do you listen?
2. Do you make appropriate eye contact?
3. Do you use verbal cues? (*"Yes, I see. Okay."*)
4. Do you use non-verbal cues (take notes, nod your head, use positive body language)?
5. Do you paraphrase or summarize your understanding of the issue? (*"What I hear you saying is...."* *"If I understand you correctly, you mean...."*)

Explore

Do you know and understand what the employee is trying to say? Use questions to better gain perspective from the customer's point of view.

1. Do you maintain your composure and stay professional?
2. Do you use open-ended questions (what, how, where, why) to gain more information?
3. Do you use closed questions (yes or no) to gain agreement or closure?
4. Do you use directives to gain additional information (*"Tell me more about...."* *"Explain that again...."* *"Talk more about...."*)?
5. Do you paraphrase again for understanding?

Attend

Are your attitude and behavior communicating that you care?

Words. Constructive, conversational, and non-confrontational language. This equals 7 percent of your communication impact.

Tone of voice. Maintain a similar tone of voice as the employee. This equals 38 percent of your communication result.

Physiology. Ensure that your actions and body language are congruent with a genuine desire to be of service. This measures 55 percent of your communication power.[1]

1. Do you maintain your focus on the employee by holding on to your response until you have gained understanding?
2. Do you pay attention to the employee's demeanor and emotions?
3. Do you ask more clarifying questions, if needed?

Define a Solution

Notice that, up to this point, you focus on understanding the issue, gaining employee input, and dealing with any emotional response. Before you respond and finalize a plan, you may have to listen, explore, and attend multiple times. It depends on the complexity of the problem and the depth of the employee's emotional response. After this you define specific actions or solutions.

1. Do you summarize your understanding?
2. Do you specifically respond and give feedback?
3. Do you work with the employee to outline possible alternative solutions?
4. Do you close for agreement on the issue, on next steps, or for the business?

LEAD

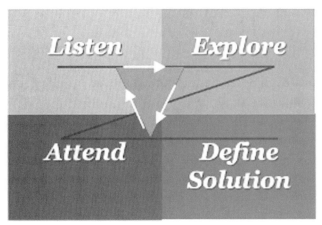

The Review With LEAD method provides balance among asking for input, listening effectively to employee ideas, and responding and creating solutions to the issue. It allows for your employee and you to "unpack" emotional responses constructively. Finally, it ensures a focused response that is more likely to address the employee's true problem. Graphically, the LEAD model is represented here. Notice that the process is iterative, with repetitive attention to the Listen, Explore, and Attend steps to ensure precise identification of the employee's concerns before an attempt is made to define the solution.

Reprimand

The term *reprimand* strikes fear in the hearts of some managers, especially in this day and age of employee rights, legislative human resources policies, and a lawsuit-happy society. Others find it a joy to do. Both are extremes. Reprimands have a bad rap because of a few bad managers who scream at employees for poor performance.

Effective reprimands can be powerful motivation tools and help employees correct their course to improve results. First, only give reprimands to experienced employees. The only exception has to do with any issues related to societal laws or company policies that are deliberately or blatantly violated. Second, use Review With LEAD as a precursor to a reprimand. Continue the LEAD process several times as long as the employee seems to be making a reasonable effort. Use your judgment here, because there are no ironclad rules. If you have provided the employee with clear expectations and goals, ongoing coaching, recognition or praise, regular and effective training, and proactive and supportive communication, and performance still suffers, use the reprimand. Here's how a reprimand works:

- ▶ Do your homework, and have all your information at hand.
- ▶ Know that a reprimand is not a dialogue or a long, drawn-out meeting. It's largely one-way, short, and to the point. Meet with the employee privately.
- ▶ Be immediate after the lack of performance surfaces.
- ▶ Be specific, and describe the specific performance problem. (*"Sue, you did not complete the customer visitations we discussed."*)

▶ Share your feelings of disappointment or anger about the lack of results. You don't have to yell or swear. You can raise your voice just a bit higher or lower than normal for emphasis. (*"I'm really disappointed that you didn't complete the report as we discussed and agreed to."*)

▶ Explain what you want and the consequences for a lack of performance. However, pause before you give the consequences. Many times, employees will apologize for letting you down and immediately perform better. If you don't receive something like this, give the consequences. (*"I expect you to make the calls we agreed to, or I will give you a written warning."*)

▶ Reaffirm the person. Remember: This is an experienced person who has received lots of help to do a better job. Most often, the lack of performance is an issue of a lack of follow-through on past agreements. It's usually not a skill issue but a matter of will or "want to." (*"I know you can make this happen. You have in the past. You just need to act on the plan."*)

A reprimand won't take but a few minutes. Don't get into a debate; ask the employee to follow the plan you have already discussed. Make sure to follow up later to check on results. If the employee has made progress, praise the effort, even if it isn't perfect. If not, carry through on the consequences.

Note: These methods of dealing with performance problems are proactive approaches designed to help an employee succeed. When dealing with performance issues that reoccur, follow your company policies and seek additional advice from your manager or human resources. Do this proactively, not as a last resort. Document your performance discussions, and never be judgmental in your descriptions. Focus on the performance issue. (For example: The employee made 10 mistakes out of 15 tries compared to a quality goal of one or less. Not: The employee is stupid because of all of the mistakes.)

Day 6 Superstar Leader Application
What two to three ideas did you learn from this section on dealing with performance problems?
Think of a situation where you can apply each of the three methods. How will you do each?
Redirect.
Review With LEAD.
Reprimand.

Every job is a self-portrait of the person who did it. Autograph your work with excellence.

—Jessica Guidobono

COMMUNICATING POSITIVELY AND PROACTIVELY

DAY 7: Communicating Respectfully

DAY 8: Effective People Skills

DAY 9: Mental Models

DAY 10: Handling Conflict

Day 7
COMMUNICATING
RESPECTFULLY

We live in a diverse world. A Superstar leader accepts the richness of that diversity and treats all people with respect and dignity at all times. For the best bosses, workplace communication is free from prejudice and discrimination, and does not include racial slurs or off-colored humor. The worst bosses disregard the need for respectful communication through ignorance or blatant denial of its necessity. Disrespect toward others, implied or explicit, will negate everything else you might do well as a boss.

Building Awareness

In today's society, it is hard to miss diversity. Many communities are a "rainbow coalition" of people from all walks of life, from all over the world. In the workplace, both customers and employees mirror this diversity. As a result, managers have a critical responsibility to model respect and acceptance, which their employees can emulate. Your actions, as the adage says, will speak louder than your words.

Communication is easier today than ever with cell phones, e-mail, networking Websites, and the ability to connect at any time with minimal effort. Whether we fly overseas, make a phone call, or interact through a videoconference, we can meet new people from different cultures with ease. Yet, it is not quite so easy to melt away the distrust and prejudice that sometimes accompanies cross-cultural interaction.

In the 1940s, Abraham Maslow identified a hierarchy of human needs that applies to everyone: physical care and safety, social acceptance, mental growth, and a sense of purpose/fulfillment.[1] Even in the 21st century, people have the same basic set of needs, whether they are short, tall, male, female, black, white, Catholic, Methodist, Muslim, Spanish, Japanese, manager, or employee. Superstar leaders understand that people are still people—no matter their diverse characteristics—and treat them equally well.

Superstar leaders know that the greatest resource of a business is its people. They recognize the value of diversity when people work together; there will be new and better ideas, more depth of perception and ingenuity, increased quality in customer service, and better productivity.

On the following chart, circle the areas that have affected your own experiences (add your own ideas as applicable).

People are different in:	People are similar in needing:	People are similar in wanting:
Political beliefs	Physical care/safety	Social justice
Social status	Social acceptance	Equal opportunity
Cultural norms	Mental growth	Political rights
Ethnic backgrounds	Sense of purpose/ fulfillment	Education access
Religious beliefs	Respect and courtesy	Religious freedom
Other:	Other:	Other:

Accepting Diversity

In many instances across businesses, diversity training has become a legislated reality because people fail to accept one another by their own initiative; they fail to understand that differences are not something to fear. As a result, it is unlawful, and simply not right, to discriminate, show prejudice, or practice harassment toward others in our society.

Companies are required by law to implement policies and procedures that support discrimination laws and protect both employees and customers. Managers who strongly support diversity are assets to a company and contribute to a collaborative company climate. Those who don't are expendable, a liability to their companies, as they sow discontent and hatred.

From the perspective of the Superstar leader, accepting the differences among people comes from within, not from a law or policy. Acceptance extends from the heart as the Superstar leader communicates with every customer, coworker, or employee with courtesy, respect, dignity, and care. A good leader works to understand differences, not eliminate them.

Superstar leaders move from "heart" acceptance to "hands-on" action, helping their employees become the best they can be. A good employee is a reflection of a good boss; success reflects success as both customers and the company are well served. A good leader gives every employee the same opportunity to succeed or helps find their niche elsewhere.

Complete the diversity exercise to help you evaluate your acceptance skills.

The Diversity Exercise
Think of a person with whom you have a hard time working, particularly someone with a cultural background, ethnicity, or values that differ from your own. Describe that person in as much detail as you can, based on the following list, and then answer the questions that follow.
1. Interests or hobbies.
2. Career experience.
3. Education background.
4. Family.
5. Strengths.
6. Weaknesses.
7. Personal goals.
8. Likes/dislikes.
9. Favorite recreation/music/food.
10. Dream vacation.
How well do you really know or understand this person? (Note: Oftentimes our lack of understanding and knowledge is the problem not the person.)
How can you accept and work more effectively with this person? (Note: This is about changes you can make.)

Managing Diversity

Superstar leaders can learn to masterfully manage diversity among employees, and create positive and motivating work environments. However, they often first see themselves in the mirror and realize, "The enemy is me."

To effectively influence others, Superstar leaders understand they must first manage their own perceptions. Many managers discover, through diversity exercises such as the previous one, that they do not know their coworkers as well as they thought. They learn that their critical assumptions and judgments about others arise out of a lack of understanding or learned biases and prejudice.

But perceptions can change. By using a tool called PACT, you can more positively manage diversity. Rate your performance for each statement, and then answer the questions to improve your PACT with others.

1	2	3	4	5

Very Infrequently   Very Frequently

☐ P: Practice being polite, respectful, and helpful with all people (for example, no rude jokes or offensive stories allowed).

☐ A: Accept the differences in others without judgments. Accept the similarities, too.

☐ C: Collaborate and communicate with all people by being a good listener.

☐ T: Treat all people with dignity, fairness, and equal opportunity.

How well do you really manage diversity? (Note: Oftentimes our lack of understanding and knowledge is the problem, not other people.)
How can you accept and work more effectively with others in today's diverse workplace? (Note: This is about changes you can make.)

Taking Positive Action

A large agricultural company in the United States was trying to work a deal with a multinational company from Spain. Soon after introductions were made, the U.S. executives wanted to get approval on a contract. The Spanish executives were puzzled and asked the interpreter what was going on. The U.S. executives did not understand that Spanish culture presumes that the parties will take time to talk, eat together, and get to know each other better before conducting business. The U.S. managers did not determine their cross-cultural differences beforehand and, as a result, did not manage diversity or communicate effectively.

Businesspeople worldwide acknowledge the positive and powerful force of accepting and managing diversity, a lesson learned by adoption agencies that regularly connect people from different cultures. These agencies have shown that disadvantaged children who are adopted and brought into loving and caring yet culturally different homes can overcome tremendous obstacles. The adoption process is predicated on the wisdom of a simple philosophy: love one another. Businessman and author Bob Conklin restated this philosophy for the work world as follows:

▶ Give other people what they need and you'll get what you need.

▶ Help others be successful and you'll be successful.[2]

Superstar leaders embrace the concepts of diversity and use them as a basis for more effective communication. As a result, those bosses are proven genuine and credible.

Day 7 Superstar Leader Application
What can you learn from the discussion on diversity?
How have you done this in the past?
What positive changes will you make to achieve better results?

All excellence is equally difficult!

—Author Unknown

Day 8
EFFECTIVE PEOPLE
SKILLS

Effective leaders inspire others to be their best. The ability to influence others requires superb communication skills. CEOs, when asked, regularly attribute their success to their strong communication skills. Employees, conversely, regularly complain about the lack of communication in their workplaces. What a difference in perceptions!

Talk about productivity, finances, and numbers is usually termed a hard skill that managers need. Working with people, on the other hand, is often considered a soft skill. This is where most managers are gravely mistaken. There is nothing soft about human relationships. The complexities of psychological makeup and emotional intricacies multiply as work groups get bigger. The web of human relationships creates the perfect breeding ground for Superstar leaders to practice and improve their people skills.

Many bosses don't seem to care how they communicate. Superstar-leaders are deeply committed to working effectively with those they lead, developing strong people skills in themselves and others. The dynamics of human relationships can make or break a company. A good boss will learn how to use those dynamics to support the company's goals, build confidence in themselves and others, and create a strong working environment. Effective leaders have effective people skills, and it's as much a part of their character as it is their skill at "active leadership communication."[1] There are two crucial elements to developing people skills and building confidence: the communication climate and effective listening.

People Skill Element #1: Communication Climate

To succeed as a manager, don't do what every other manager does. Expand your comfort zone; don't stay within the mold, as Tom Peters suggests in his book, *Liberation Management*.[2] In other words, challenge your mental models, which we will discuss in Day 9.

A manager at a large textile rental company made this comment after one of our Excellence in Management seminars: "I asked the other managers at our company if they knew the leadership skills we learned and applied. They said they knew some of them. But you know what? They never use them."

Knowledge is not power. Acting on the knowledge is power. To become a good boss or a Superstar leader, you have to be willing to do what others don't do or are too lazy to do well. Superstar leaders are willing to find ways to improve and communicate more effectively, to move from good to excellent. Poor bosses don't care how they communicate; for them, good is good enough, or their only goal is to get what they want.

A communication climate is created the second two people start to interact. Sometimes it's positive, and other times it's negative. The communication climate is often like the weather: You can find clues as to what is happening by carefully observing the signs. If the sky is blue, it's 80 degrees, and there's a light breeze, you can picture the pleasant day. On the other hand, if the humidity is skyrocketing and black clouds begin to swirl in the distance, you know you'd best get ready to take cover from the pending storm. A communication climate can be similarly detected, and what it reveals will affect how people get along.

The communication climate is more behavioral than attitudinal in orientation; it is determined by what people do, either positive actions or negative actions. Most of us do some of each as we talk to another person. What matters is if we do more positive or negative behaviors. What matters most is if we intend to be helpful or hurtful. Positive or negative. Confrontational or a problem-solver. The good news is that actions can be managed. How do we manage this? We focus our intentions and change our behavior appropriately, hopefully more positively. This, in turn, helps others to change or improve their actions.

Consider this example. You are talking to an employee about a workplace problem. You rarely make eye contact, and you shuffle papers and read e-mail documents throughout your conversation. How might the employee feel?

Then consider a conversation with a customer. You welcome him into your office, offer him a cup of coffee, sit together at a table, and look at him with concern as you discuss business needs. Which set of behavior will achieve more favorable results?

We can control the communication climate by communicating in consistently positive ways. The immediate outcome when working with employees is higher employee satisfaction and high-quality customer service at every level.

A good leader will consciously contribute in a positive manner to the communication climate of any interaction. There are several key considerations when trying to create a good communication climate:

▸ Your behavior is of critical priority. You can't control what the other person does. You can only control your own actions.

▸ Remember that all behaviors are either positive or negative, and rarely neutral, in their impact.

▸ In any given situation, you don't always know what actions will make a difference. You may not know how you are coming across to others.

▸ By becoming more aware of what contributes to a positive or a negative climate, you can make changes to be more effective. Become more aware by paying attention to how others react to you.

▸ You can manage the communication climate by changing your behavior as the situation dictates.

For example, Pete is a service manager in a highly competitive industry. He manages reps that sell business-to-business products. He works hard and is genuinely concerned about employees and customers. His major challenge is high employee turnover. Just when he seems to have his department clicking, he loses people. Pete is intense, and he wants things done his way. If things are not done his way, he often jumps in and does it himself. He criticizes employees for what wasn't done to his satisfaction; he doesn't take the time to train or coach them. His employees end up resentful and, in time, they get frustrated and quit. Pete thinks he is doing all he can because he works so hard. Pete has to improve his communication skills and coaching skills to keep people on board, and to reach the next level in results. Do the Communication Climate Checklist Exercise as you consider how to create a positive communication climate.

Communication Climate Checklist Exercise

DIRECTIONS: Circle five behaviors in the "POSITIVE" column that you need to start or continue. Circle three behaviors in the "NEGATIVE" column that you need to avoid. What steps can you take to eliminate the negative behaviors? How can you use your strengths more effectively?

POSITIVE	NEGATIVE
Listen (restate the problem).	Avoid eye contact.
Make eye contact.	Act hostile.
Sit up straight.	Allow interruptions.
Use the person's name.	Eliminate physical barriers, such as a desk.
Allow no interruptions.	Answer questions with a question.
Give full attention.	Watch the clock.
Ask questions.	Act defensive.
Smile.	Frown.
Use firm handshake.	Slouch.
Give compliments.	Use monotone voice.
Be courteous.	Be insincere.
Take notes.	Don't follow through.
Use verbal cues, such as "*I see.*"	Use bad language.
Act enthusiastic.	Be sarcastic.
Make a decision.	Have a sloppy appearance.
Stay on subject.	Rush the problem/person.
Encourage the person.	Talk about personal problems.
Eliminate barriers.	Criticize others.
Do something extra.	Other
Stay positive.	
Other	

People Skill Element #2: Effective Listening

We worked with Bob Conklin, successful salesman, businessman, and motivator, for five years. He said in a meeting, "To listen, you must want to listen." Listening is the first ingredient of effective communication. Do you care enough to pay attention?

Superstar leaders are good listeners. They take time to tune in to the problems of subordinates, coworkers, or customers. They are willing to overcome the many barriers to effective listening. Look at the following list, and note the items that affect your attempts to listen effectively. Which three do you let get in the way of your communication?

▸ Your ideas or experience.

▸ People or phone interruptions.

▸ Differences of opinion.

▸ Prejudices or biases.

▸ Conflict of priorities.

▸ Perception of the problems or situation.

▸ Lack of interest.

▸ Limited time.

▸ Thinking about other things.

▸ Formulating a response.

▸ Thinking the speaker is wrong.

▸ Your mood.

▸ Knowledge, facts, and information of the situation.

Being a great communicator and listening are hard work, and consequently many people, including managers, fail at it. It is in a manager's best interest to work on developing good listening skills; poor communication costs businesses billions of dollars each year in lost performance and related morale problems. Employees often feel unappreciated because they believe no one listens to them or cares.

Superstar leaders want to listen and make the conscious choice to do so. There are useful techniques that support that choice. Consider the following key elements of effective listening:

Eye Contact

In Japan, eye contact is limited. You want to look down and not lock eyeballs. In the Middle East, eye contact is more intense and direct; it's expected. In the United States, eye contact is called the glance-away method. You look at someone for three to four seconds and look away. Making eye contact is appropriate, but you don't want to stare; it's intimidating. Appropriate eye contact expresses interest and concern. You can also observe how a person is responding to you.

Proper eye contact expresses interest, respect, and empathy. A skilled listener will become adroit at making eye contact without making others uncomfortable. Eye contact will make people feel special and that they really matter.

Finding Common Ground

A successful salesperson once explained his achievements this way: "I like to find common ground or interest with everyone. If people like movies, we talk about the current hits. If they are into sports, so am I. If they have kids, I become one of the family. I'm like a chameleon."

Establishing connections through common ground or interests is a key to influencing others. Superstar leaders take the time to discover the things that interest their employees, including their backgrounds, family, and career paths. Those interests become part of the conversations with employees.

Remembering Body Language

We have discussed and referenced this earlier in dealing with performance issues. Dr. Albert Mehrabian did the initial studies that indicated three areas that have the greatest effect on good communication:

1. Words—what we say!
2. Tone of voice—how we say it!
3. Body language—what we do as we say it and after we say it![3]

As a listener, your body movements will convey how well you are listening and whether you mean what you say. Your movements express your concern and willingness to be involved. Lean forward and toward the speaker. Face the person directly. Don't fold your arms; keep them on your lap or desk. Take notes if appropriate. (Ask permission first.) Put your feet flat on the floor.

As noted previously, your words account for 7 percent of your communication impact. Your tone of voice accounts for 38 percent. Body language, however, influences communication by an amazing 55 percent. What you say is one thing. How you say it is also significant. But, what you do as you communicate is most powerful. An effective strategy for effective listening, and communication overall, is to match the speaker's body language. Sit when she sits; cross your arms if she does. Subtly—do not mimic—mirror the speaker's gestures and shifts in position. Taking these postures will convey the message that "You can trust me; I'm like you!"

Using People's Names

People love hearing their name; it is a sweet sound. By using a person's name, the individual hears you almost immediately; you will also grab a person's attention. It is personable and expresses genuineness.

Paraphrasing

Paraphrasing what you've heard is an appropriate response to large quantities of information. By putting what you've heard into your own words—repeating what you've been told—you will not only remember the information better, but also the speaker will know that you were listening. Clarifications can also be made if you have misunderstood something.

Begin a paraphrase by saying something such as *"If I understand you correctly"* or *"What I hear you saying is."*

Avoid bland phrases such as *"I understand"* or *"I know what you mean."* Also avoid saying, *"What you really mean is...."* This can be construed as condescending or trying to put words in the speaker's mouth.

The Goal of Listening

The primary goal of listening is not necessarily agreement; it's understanding. As you listen more closely, you will better understand others, and they will seek more to understand you because of your efforts. Listening effectively will make a positive impact. You will learn new things about people and your operation. You will become a better boss. Of course, there are others ways to listen to your team besides the skills we have described: team meetings, attitude surveys, observing team interaction, focus groups, and action teams. (We will comment on these in Day 9.)

Poor bosses go through the motions of "listening" merely to obtain agreement or to manipulate people to do things their way; they are not striving for understanding. Through time, this will become a hollow effort and will destroy credibility and trust.

Excellence in Communication

Dr. Daniel Goleman, author of several books on emotional intelligence, suggests that effective people skills are about the mastery of self and relationships with others. His research shows that business success often comes down to relationship skills, and, because most managers feel they have effective people skills, they don't spend much time trying to develop better skills.[4]

A convention speaker asked the members of his audience to stand if they couldn't get along with other people. No one stood up. After a long silence, a young man finally stood up in the back of the room.

The speaker asked, "Young man, you mean to tell me that you can't get along with other people?"

The man replied, "Oh, sure I can. But I felt sorry for you standing up there all by yourself."

Poor people skills—not getting along—are a result of people not working at these skills or not knowing how to work on them or what to work on. People are generally selfish, looking out for number one, and many people lack the confidence or sense of security that helps them get along well with others.

How, then, can managers better communicate and motivate people who generally have poor people skills or only look out for number one?

Successful communication starts with an attitude we stated in Day 7: Give other people what they want, and you'll get what you want. Notice that first you give, and then you get. It doesn't happen the other way around. This age-old Golden Rule applies in any relationship and any organization.

Tom Peters, coauthor of the book *In Search of Excellence,* found that when people tried to identify policies, structures, and procedures that made a company great, they instead found intangibles that most affected company success. They discovered characteristics such as enthusiasm, pride, respect, caring, fun, and love.[5]

To influence or communicate effectively with people, you have to give more, and you may need to develop a stronger sense of giving. These simple rules may help you build positive relationships with people:

▸ People who are alike tend to enjoy each other and work well together.

▸ People who are different tend to dislike each other and not work well together.

▸ Give other people what they want, and you will get what you want.

▸ Be genuine in dealing with all people.

In most cases, you will find yourself with some differences from those with whom you work. In this day and age of diverse work environments, you might have coworkers from all around the world. Your backgrounds and perspectives on life could be vastly different. Regardless of where you are from, you need to communicate better with people from all walks of life to be an effective leader. How do you work with others? Learn to adapt. Be sensitive to their needs, skills, likes, and dislikes so that you can influence them more positively. Businessman Warren Buffet said, "It takes twenty years to build a reputation and five minutes to ruin it. If you think about that, you'll do things differently."[6]

The following example illustrates two strategies that help you be a good leader with effective people skills.

A manager took a job as an executive with a new company in a different industry. His job required interaction and cooperation from management across departments and divisions, even though he had little experience in the industry. He set two immediate goals: create positive relationships around the organization, and demonstrate competence and credibility through small wins.

Early on, he met one-on-one with all division managers in their own offices; he listened to their needs and concerns. Additionally, he soon made a few immediate-impact decisions that showed the managers that he could add value to their businesses. This manager built partnerships across the company and, to make a long story short, the other managers collaborated with him to significantly improved service, quality, and sales.

Superstar leaders understand the value of people skills, recognize the differences in people, and work hard to communicate genuinely and professionally. Superstar leaders avoid intimidation or political intrigue, which alienates people and negatively affects their performance. Superstar leaders become students of effective communication and consistently strive to improve their people skills.

Day 8 Superstar Leader Application
What did you learn from the discussion on effective people skills?
What are your strongest people skills?
What positive changes will you make to achieve better results?

Management is doing things right; leadership is doing the right things.

—Peter F. Drucker

Day 9
MENTAL MODELS

We all have our own way of looking at the world, or our unique perception of life and its possibilities or problems. We call this our mental models.

Mental models are influenced by our family background, religion, race, socio-economic status, experiences, goals, gender, needs, fears, beliefs, and dreams. Look at the following and note your answers alongside each, or just mentally log your responses. (Note: These images are from the Mighty Optical Illusions Website, *www.moillusions.com*.)

What do you see?

What do you see?

There's a face and the word liar.

Do you see three faces?

What does the sign say?   What do you see?

Are you sure?   Do you see a musician
                     or a girl's face?

Mental Math

Do this simple math problem in your head. No pencil, paper, or calculator.

> Take 1,000 and add 40 to it.
> Now add another 1,000.
> Now add another 30.
> Now add another 1,000.
> Now add 20.
> Now add another 1,000.
> Now add 10.
> What is the total?

Did you get 5,000? Circle YES or NO.

Now add the numbers on paper with a pencil.

What dynamic is at play here?

Perception—our mental models. The answer is actually 4,100.

We don't all see things the same way. Our perceptions, or mental models, of the world and how we interpret situations or problems differ from one person to another. This is sadly illustrated year after year by the ongoing Middle East conflict. For hundreds of years, countries in that region have faced the same conflicts; they never seem willing or able to understand each other's point of view. They cannot comprehend each other's mental model.

The fact of business life is that managers often face the same dilemma, not always seeing what is there. Managers sometimes fail to see the "obvious" opportunities, problems, and solutions. Our visual exercise demonstrated how our perceptions vary. Superstar leaders find ways to adjust their mental models; bad bosses hold fast to their own ways of thinking and shut out others' ideas. They get stuck in a box.

In his book, *The Fifth Discipline*, Peter Senge suggests that in leadership, the ability to achieve a desired result is often eroded by our perception that our own beliefs are the truth, that the truth is obvious, that our beliefs are based on real data, and that the data we select are the real data.[1] Leadership is not about having all the answers and solutions for the problems facing a department or company. Leadership is about motivating people to be innovative and committed to finding breakthrough solutions for those problems. Leadership is about positively influencing people to achieve greatness.

Great leadership is about influencing great performance in other people. Superstar leaders leverage their successes accordingly; ineffective bosses attempt to do it all on their own.

Ask yourself these questions:

▸ Are you stuck in a box, holding tightly to your own perceptions?

▸ Do you have a hard time getting things done or keeping pace with your business?

▸ Do you seem to have the same problems over and over?

▸ Do you have a hard time motivating your employees to perform more effectively and sustain that trend?

▸ Does your team seem to lack new ideas and solutions?

▸ Do employees seem to lack the ability to take initiative in problem-solving?

If you answered yes to some or all of these, you may be stuck and lack an open mind. Many of the strategies discussed thus far will enhance your leadership abilities, if you consistently implement them, but you have to make some changes and be open-minded. Consider one more important strategy illustrated by the following two examples.

A new sales manager in a car dealership faced sluggish sales and pressure from the dealership's owner to improve them. The sales manager gathered his sales reps and threatened to fire them if they did not each sell 10 units. He boasted to the owner about how he "motivated his troops." Within two months, the sales manager was out the door himself because sales had not improved.

Jim is a manager at a Canadian company in Winnipeg. His team's performance began to deteriorate because of new competition and employee turnover. Jim tried to pick up the slack himself, following through on customer requests and sales, but he was soon overwhelmed. After talking to WCW Partners and gaining some ideas, support, and insight, Jim chose to make three adjustments. First, he held a team meeting, explained the situation, and asked for help and ideas. The group brainstormed ways to be more efficient and respond to the new competitive market. Second, Jim met with employees individually to discuss their situations, goals, and educational needs for the job. Third, Jim did more coaching and kicked off a new promotion/incentive for his team based on their input. Within a few weeks, performance began to improve and ultimately exceeded the team's accomplishments prior to the changes.

Where did the first sales manager fail? What did Jim do differently? Jim listened and brought the team together to help deal with the challenges he faced. The first sales manager used unproductive threats and never discussed the situation with his sales reps.

Although our society tends to reward leaders who seem to have all the answers and take swift action, those who are truly successful may not act as swiftly and may need to admit they do not have all the answers. The most effective leaders will listen first and then respond, organizationally as well as interpersonally. Listening in the broader sense will help us feel the pulse of the organization and what's happening with customers and employees alike.

This means tapping into the collective intellectual power of an entire team to solve problems. It means adjusting our mental models to include other people's perceptions, input, ideas, and solutions, not just our own. Superstar leaders are open to this type of information exchange; bad bosses are not. Poor bosses let their egos get in the way and say, "It's my way or the highway." So how do you implement this strategy? Consider these steps as a way to widen, or significantly expand, your mental models:

1. Improve your one-on-one listening skills and hold regular (weekly or monthly) team meetings to talk about how your team is doing. One manager said he didn't need such meetings because everyone talked every day. Though that may be true, the conversations are typically reactive to the issues of the day. Regular team meetings are proactive, designed to create a synergy through thinking together, as a team. They also help everyone feel more committed to and involved in the team's overall results because they become part of the solution, not just the brunt of finger-pointing.

2. Include your team in annual planning meetings. Do this for same reasons you hold weekly or monthly meetings. Let the team help you set an agenda for the year—goals and actions steps.

3. Conduct brainstorming sessions. When particularly tough problems arise, brainstorm ideas together. Remember that in brainstorming, all ideas are good ideas. Set a five- to 10-minute time limit, get everyone to write down their own ideas first, share the ideas around the room, and do not evaluate any ideas; just list them on a flipchart for all to see. Then, as a group, prioritize the ideas. Use these for your plans.

4. Hold feedback sessions. Take time to simply listen to your employees. For example, Dave ran a very successful business, leading his industry and market in sales, customer satisfaction, and profit. Twice yearly, he held meetings with each department and asked for feedback. No matter what was said during those meeting, he just took notes. Following those meetings, he set aside office hours for employees to come and talk to him. Again, he listened. After a few weeks, he would again meet with each department and summarize what he had heard during the feedback sessions and individual meetings, and then described the changes he would make and what would remain the same. He gained the respect of his employees and managers.

5. Form action teams. Form small groups of four to six employees, and give them a problem to solve with a time limit. Document those solutions, and implement their ideas. We worked with a team to help a truck manufacturer in their drive to improve customer satisfaction. They used action teams at their dealerships and significantly improved service, eventually earning them the JD Power Award for customer satisfaction.

6. Survey employees. A few times a year, survey employees to gain insight into your department or a particular problem. Surveys can be related to sales promotions, training needs, customer service issues, cost-saving ideas, and more. Always report back to people what you heard and what you will do in response.

7. Do a leadership inventory. Allow your employees, coworkers, and boss(es) to rate your leadership skills. To be most effective, use an outside source to keep it anonymous. (For example, WCW Partners conducts these ratings for customers.) These ratings can prove invaluable to help you get beyond your personal mental models to improve your leadership, listening, and management efforts.

8. One manager who believed he was an excellent coach received a 50/50 split rating from 10 of his direct reports. He discovered that he was working with all his employees the same way but only meeting the coaching needs of half of them. He was consequently able to tailor his approach to meet the needs, goals, skills, and desires of the other half as well.

9. Keep learning. Author Stephen Covey says to continually sharpen the saw.[2] Participate in ongoing training regularly to learn new skills, as well as to discover new ideas that can open your mind. Superstar leaders make it a point to attend three to five training sessions a year. Bad bosses keep doing the same things over and over and are resistant to anything new; they dig a deeper pit. An old proverb says that unless we keep changing, we grow hard and stale.

Day 9 Superstar Leadership Application
What can you learn from the discussion on mental models?
In what areas might you be most rigid in your approach to your job and employees?
Which method or two will you use to get outside the box and to open your mind?

To be all we can be, we must dream of being more!

—Anonymous

Day 10
HANDLING CONFLICT

Contrary to popular opinion, conflict is good. A manager without occasional conflict within his team lacks real credibility. Conflict arises from a variety of sources:

▶ Differences of opinion.

▶ Problem-solving.

▶ Human resources issues.

▶ Performance problems.

▶ Interpersonal issues.

▶ Customer complaints.

▶ Decision-making.

Conflict is always present, whether or not you recognize it, but conflict does not have to be negative. How you handle conflict greatly influences your team's cohesiveness and ability to work together effectively. Superstar leaders deal with conflict constructively and create trust, credibility, and rapport with their team. Bad bosses avoid or dismiss conflict and subsequently denigrate their integrity and that of the team.

Why is it important to deal with conflict? Primarily because it is the honest thing to do. People don't always agree with each other; conflict is inevitable. Yet conflict doesn't require that people fight, yell, or scream at one another. If you want healthy and positive working relationships, conflict requires that you communicate and work through problems.

Conflict management is modeled by the team leader—by you, the boss. Your employees will mimic how you handle conflict. If you dismiss, avoid, or excessively delay dealing with conflict, your team members will likewise be hesitant to address issues. Unresolved conflict usually results in problems that fester and get worse, weakened communication, destroyed trust, and ineffective performance.

By dealing with conflict quickly and effectively, you create an atmosphere that promotes positive communication, and increases the quality and efficiency of your work. When issues are brought out in the open, they don't have a chance to fester. Input is heard, decisions are made, people feel better, and things get done more quickly.

How does a good boss effectively handle conflict? Start by letting your team members know you value open communication. Let team members know you want to hear about their issues and problems, and let them know you want—and expect—them to offer solutions as well. Communicate this openness early and often in your work relationships.

Next, openly and constructively address the issues you observe. If an employee does something you don't like, approach the subject and state the issue without being judgmental. For example, say, *"Bill, I noticed you changed the procedure we have for handling customer complaints. Tell me about your plan."* An inquiry such as this gives Bill a chance to explain his motivation and intentions. Similarly, if employees deliver bad news or report on a problem, remain objective and thank them for the information. Don't "shoot the messenger" who brings negative information.

Disagreements between employees require some careful handling. Here are some suggestions:

> If it is a cordial disagreement, allow them to continue without intervention. Be available as a good listener or to ask questions that help clarify the problem. Don't take sides, and be sure to apply the people skills you've acquired.

> If the disagreement is not cordial, intervene and discuss ways to deal with the issue constructively. Facilitate by asking the parties to state their ideas and ask them to paraphrase each other's perspectives. Another intervention may be to require a cooling down period, after which they meet again (possibly with you) to resolve the problem.

Gloria and Mark were managers who didn't work well together; they didn't like each other, either. They constantly bickered about work goals and procedures. Nearly every week, they would individually go to their boss, Shirley, to complain about each other. Shirley listened, and encouraged them to focus on the business problems and try to work together as teammates, but as months went on there was no improvement. When their issues bubbled over in a staff meeting, Shirley brought the two together for a separate meeting. She reprimanded them for allowing their differences to disrupt the staff meeting. She reiterated her expectations for allowing staff members to do things differently within set protocols. She also restated their department value of teamwork.

Shirley asked both managers to state their issues. She listened empathetically to their concerns and positions. Together, they problem-solved ways to deal with each other effectively, and Shirley asked them to commit to working on their business relationship. They agreed. Although they didn't always agree with each other, from then on, they addressed their issues and worked together in the best interests of their department and customers, and problems were minimized.

The primary goal of conflict management is to create a positive and productive working environment. There are two main methodologies for managing conflict that do not squelch performance or break trust:

1. **The LEAD model.** As mentioned in Day 6, this is a key method for dealing with performance issues and conflict management.

2. **Constructive confrontation.** Use this method if the LEAD model is not effective in resolving conflict.

The LEAD Model

The goal is a win/win resolution to the problem. A good boss starts with being a good listener, paraphrasing concerns, asking probing questions to gain a clearer understanding, attending to the emotional state of the person(s) with the problem, and, finally, defining a game plan or solution. You might have to work through this process multiple times before obtaining a workable solution to the problem.

> L—Listen.
>
> E—Explore.
>
> A—Attend.
>
> D—Define a solution.

In the previous example, Shirley effectively used this approach with the two managers. Sometimes the LEAD model doesn't work. People are people, and things don't always work out smoothly. At that point, constructive confrontation can be useful.

Constructive Confrontation

Use this approach if the conflict becomes more difficult or if those involved are unwilling to follow through on previous agreements. (This approach is used by many practitioners we have learned from. We are unaware of any single author.) This method requires a step-by-step approach using language such as these examples:

▶ "[*person's name*], I have a problem we need to talk about." (Use a collective "we" so the person listens without getting defensive.)

▶ "When you [*state the issue*], "I feel [*tell how you feel in non-judgmental language*]."

▶ "I would prefer [*tell the person how you want him or her to act*]."

▶ "If you do, [*state a positive outcome*]."

Pause to wait for a response.

Most of the time the person will become conciliatory and cooperative. If not, take the next step.

▶ "If you don't [*re-state what you want—the positive outcome*], then I will [*state a consequence for not taking the actions*]."

Here is an example:

> *"Bill, I have a problem we need to talk about. When you don't follow through with the budget numbers we need for our project, I am disappointed by your lack of support for the team. I would prefer you get me the numbers on time, as we have discussed. If you do, the entire team will be grateful and on track for reaching our goals. (Pause.) If you don't, I will need to reassign you another task and note this matter in your personnel file."*

Conflict is natural. If you deal with it constructively, you will have more effective communication with your team, and it will unleash their creative juices to solve problems. Without effective conflict management, you will be hard-pressed to build a high-performance team.

Day 10 Superstar Leader Application
Think of a boss from your past jobs that handled conflict well. What methods did he or she employ?
Think of a boss from your past jobs that didn't handle conflict well. In what ways did he or she fail?
How does your analysis relate to the discussion in this chapter?
What can you do to handle conflict more effectively?

Delegating work works; provided the one delegating works, too.

—Robert Half

COACHING FOR EXCELLENCE

Day 11
INFORMAL COACHING

Cliff was an excellent manager and had recently retired. His company used him as a troubleshooter during the latter part of his career. When asked how he achieved his success, he laughed, sat back in his chair, and put his hands behind his head. Then he abruptly leaned forward and said, "I didn't go to college."

He smiled as he continued, "Every day as I came into the office, I went out in the offices, and talked to employees and customers. I would talk to Pete about his soccer coaching or Jan about her ill grandmother or Dick about his vacation. I didn't talk about work unless they brought it up. Interacting with employees on the frontline of our service helped me understand their needs and our service levels. When I had a problem and I needed help with it, I could go to my employees—Pete, Jan, Dick, or whoever—and get the straight scoop about what was happening." He then asked, "You want to know why? Over time, we developed a positive, trusting relationship, and that was invaluable to me in running my business.... Employees could talk to me and I could talk to them."

Management guru Tom Peters coined the term for this as "Managing by Wandering Around" (MBWA).[1] Cliff said his MBWA was designed to build rapport with employees and get a feel for the business through the eyes of his employees and customers on occasion.

Even though he focused on general or personal interest issues, employees inevitably brought up business in their conversations. Poor leaders don't understand this; they view conversations about mundane, everyday things as a waste of time. Superstar leaders, however, understand that time invested in the employees themselves will improve employee performance and their service to customers.

This "wandering" is a form of informal coaching. Every interaction between bosses and their employees can be informal coaching. Informal coaching is about developing positive, constructive, and respectful relationships with employees. This is not about developing friendships, and although friendships may develop, that is not the primary goal. Superstar leaders don't look to become their employees' buddy; they strive to be high performers and effective bosses.

Your employees should be able to count on you to do the right and fair thing to manage the department or team. Superstar leaders bring out the best in their employees and help secure their jobs. If you invest time coaching your employees, they will invest more in their jobs and do whatever it takes to get their jobs done well.

Managers are under pressure today to do more with less while improving productivity, quality, service, and sales. The goal targets are becoming more difficult to hit. Managers are being called to be superstar coaches; yet Superstar leaders succeed and the other bosses do not.

Beware of the bad boss behaviors that impede effective informal coaching:

▶ You have little or no time to talk over decisions with employees.

▶ You are always in meetings.

▶ You communicate primarily via e-mail.

▶ You are unapproachable because of a negative or crabby attitude.

▶ You are too busy to listen to problems.

▶ You seldom hold department or team meetings.

▶ Your problems never seem to go away, but rather escalate.

▶ You are listening less and telling more.

▶ You seldom, if ever, meet one-on-one with your employees.

▶ You blame others for your problems.

Coaching is a way to efficiently leverage a manager's time and effort. By taking the time to informally coach, you improve business overall. Why? Because when employees get fired up about what they are doing (as a result of their interactions with you and others), they do their jobs better and go the extra mile to get their work done.

How can you be an informal coach? (Mark the methods that will work for you and add a few of your own ideas.)

☐ Greet employees daily—in person or by phone or e-mail (depending on the proximity of your employees). Greet in person if you are in the same office.

☐ Be courteous and respectful with employees.

☐ Talk to employees about non-business things.

☐ Sit in on your supervisor or managers' meetings and listen.

☐ Walk around and observe the department or business in action.

☐ Verbally praise an employee in front of a few others.

☐ Verbally praise an employee in a meeting.

☐ Send an e-mail praising an employee for results or progress.

☐ Work with employees side-by-side to complete a project.

☐ Meet with an employee in his or her office, not yours.

☐ Ask employees for input on a problem.

☐ Take an employee to lunch and engage in conversation.

☐ Never criticize a person in front of others or say negative things about other people.

☐ Thank people more for their efforts; be specific.

☐ Be honest.

☐ Follow through on employee requests, and if you can't meet a time frame, let them know.

☐ Take the time to listen to employee problems.

☐ Have a sense of humor, and don't be afraid to be the brunt of a joke.

☐ Lighten up and have some fun: jokes (in good taste), office parties, going out with employees to dinner, a ball game, or a comedy club.

☐ Apologize for a personal mistake or error.

Informal coaching is about your relationship with employees. In his book *7 Habits of Highly Effective People,* Stephen Covey talks about a person's emotional bank account being much like a real bank.[2] You put money in, and you can take money out up to the total you deposited. Informal coaching puts deposits in an employee's emotional bank account. Through day-to-day interaction throughout a period of time, informal coaching makes many deposits, and the employee/boss relationship becomes stronger.

Along the way, managers have to make difficult or unpopular decisions, work with differences of opinion, report on negative feedback from customers, and handle productivity issues, as well as other less-than-positive business matters. Employees are less likely to react negatively in these situations if their emotional bank accounts are full. If their bosses have made regular deposits into their emotional bank accounts, employees will be willing to make changes and improvements in response to the difficult situations or negative feedback. A withdrawal from their emotional bank account will not bankrupt the relationship.

However, employees with depleted emotional bank accounts will likely respond negatively or not at all. If their accounts haven't seen enough deposits, the information goes in one ear and out the other. These employees typically think they have been treated unfairly or that the problem is not theirs to fix—or that you are a jerk.

Tim worked as a sheet metal worker in a Midwest manufacturing company; he was also the union steward. A large Eastern company bought his company and immediately fired everyone but said they would hire the most senior people back at a $2-per-hour lower wage. Everyone was shocked and angry; most of the employees had worked there for 15 to 20 years, and so everyone clamored for their jobs. Tim was among those rehired.

Weeks later, when asked how it was going, Tim said it was going okay and that they were getting their hourly wages back.

This appeared to be good news, but he went on to explain, "We aren't really getting any more money. We are only working when the supervisors are around. And, they aren't around that much!"

Too many bosses seem oblivious to the needs of employees, and this type of bad-boss situation is prevalent in many U.S. businesses today. Informal coaching is yet another skill Superstar leaders use to achieve excellent and sustainable results.

Day 11 Superstar Leader Application
What objections or concerns do you have about informal coaching?
How can you limit these concerns?
What do you already do that may be considered informal coaching?
How can you be a better informal coach?

When nothing is sure, everything is possible.

—Margaret Drabble

Day 12
FORMAL COACHING

Pete was a successful manager for 20 years and had won numerous awards for sales excellence. His department always led the company and competitors alike. His staff admired and liked him, and they knew he had high expectations. He had a waiting list of people who wanted to work for him. He called us one day and said, "Business is down, my people are unmotivated, and I have all these reports to do and meetings to attend. I don't have time to spend with my people."

We responded by saying, "Then you don't have time to be a manager anymore, do you?" When he met with us, we discussed his challenges and created a plan of action. He conducted a sales meeting soon thereafter, and we were invited as guest speakers. Before the meeting began, he rearranged the meeting room into a new configuration. At the start of the meeting, he explained the situation to his sales team and identified specifics that demonstrated his belief that everyone was "down in the dumps." He proceeded to take ownership for his own actions and attitudes that may have contributed to the situation. He reminded his team of their achievements, and said, "Today is a new day."

Pete then divided the group into teams to brainstorm ideas to keep the team and company moving forward. They shared their ideas and made a plan that reflected their priorities—a plan that was agreed upon by all. I (Rick) gave a motivational talk, and Pete closed the meeting with a promise to meet with each person individually in the next several days. The group left the meeting upbeat, positive, and full of energy. Pete followed through on his commitments, and business improved immediately.

Effective leaders engage their employees. Leadership is a high-contact sport. Many CEOs today don't talk to their customers or employees. The late Sam Walton of Walmart was asked why he spent one day a week in his office and the rest of the time in his stores with employees. Mr. Walton replied that he knew that was too much time in the office, but he wasn't too old to learn to be a better manager. If you aren't meeting with employees regularly, in groups or one-on-one, you are missing a key opportunity to influence them to be more successful.

As we begin this discussion about formal coaching, consider the biggest obstacle managers face: time! It's legitimate. Everyone is busy and has many things to do. A business has three key resources with which to service its customers:

1. Capital resources—the financial/money end of the business.

2. Material resources—the products and services a business offers.

3. Human resources—the people, and the potential intellectual and personal power they represent.

The human resources—people—are the most important element of any business. People put the capital and material part of the business to work and make the creative decisions on how to do so effectively and efficiently. The question is: Why wouldn't a manager want to invest time in people? The sad reality is that too many bosses get caught up in their inflated self-importance to want to mingle or interact with employees.

One business we worked with highlighted this dilemma. After talking to employees and spending time in their work areas, they asked us to get their manager to "listen to us and see what we are trying to do." They said he spent all day sending out inflammatory e-mails and creating reports on minutia. They wanted him to open his office door, get out from behind his desk, and communicate with them.

Formal coaching in a one-on-one meeting is an effective way for managers to communicate with employees on a regular basis. A one-on-one should be done privately and can take as little as five to as much as 60 minutes, depending on employee needs. As one-on-ones become more frequent, they typically take less time.

One-on-one meetings benefit the company and its leaders for a variety of reasons. They:

▸ Promote effective communication.

▸ Aid daily performance management.

▸ Provide opportunity for training/coaching.

▸ Create an employee-boss partnership.

▸ Create an atmosphere for continuous improvement.

▸ Focus on development for the future.

▸ Help businesses and employees reach and exceed their goals.

Employees receive added benefits from one-on-one meetings as well. They:

▶ Provide an opportunity for more and better communication.

▶ Provide opportunity for more frequent and immediate recognition.

▶ Reduce job anxiety and create better feeling about the job.

▶ Head off problems.

▶ Help employees position themselves for promotions.

▶ Contribute to better working relationships.

▶ Improve personal performance.

Communication alone makes this a worthwhile process. Superstar leaders are effective communicators, and they engage their employees through one-on-one interaction. A one-on-one meeting is a focused formal coaching process. Unfortunately today it seems to be a lost art.

How often should a manager do one-on-ones? This question stirs up controversy, especially as businesses have moved toward self-directed teams and employee empowerment. Experience suggests that the greater the number of customer interactions an employee has, the more frequently you need to have one-on-ones. Some businesses do them daily because their employees are talking to 50 to 200 customers a day. This kind of activity creates a sense of urgency, priority, and complexity that one-on-ones can address so customers are consistently served well. In this type of environment, one-on-ones are shorter in length. Other companies do one-on-ones weekly or monthly because the employees have less customer contact. The one-on-ones are longer in these situations (30 to 60 minutes). You will have to gauge your needs based on your particular situation.

You can expect positive results from an investment in one-on-one coaching:

▶ Met or exceeded employee goals.

▶ Greater employee input and innovation.

▶ Higher employee satisfaction.

▶ Higher-quality products.

▶ Increased customer satisfaction.

▶ Better sales, profit, and expense control.

Let your employees know your expectations for a one-on-one meeting. When planning the meeting, let them know they should be prepared to do the following:

▸ Discuss goals/activity/results.

▸ Discuss future action plans.

▸ Provide solutions to each problem or challenge.

▸ Stay positive and be respectful.

One-on-ones are successful if managers follow through on their commitments and create time in their schedules to be available to employees. This requires organization as well as contingency plans when things don't go as expected. Managers need to take and keep good notes from employee one-on-ones, and stay abreast of the metrics and goals for each employee and department. When plans change or a meeting has to be cancelled, immediate follow-up is important; if necessary, another manager can be asked to check in with the employees.

Although it is less personal, one-on-ones can be done by phone if you are separated by distance. In many of our consulting partnerships, we work with managers primarily by phone and e-mail. We conduct meetings in person two or three times per year but use phone coaching between times.

During a regional training session for a large retailer, we asked the 30 district managers to call their store managers and coach them on their customer service plans. We gave the managers talking points for these calls and then sent them off; together, they called nearly 300 stores in about 60 minutes. Following their calls, we debriefed these managers and discovered an amazing phenomenon: The store managers most often asked "What's wrong?" when they learned that their district manager was calling.

Sadly, the district managers knew the reason for this response. They typically didn't call their store managers unless there was a problem. As the district managers continued with their positive interactions, they were gratified to hear how the store managers appreciated the calls and support received during the conversations.

As a result of this exercise, the district managers continued the positive interactions with their managers throughout the next quarter, and customer service ratings soared to record levels. In addition, relationships began to improve with the stores.

A one-on-one is essentially conducted in the same manner on the phone as in person. A manager is responsible for the following:

▸ Be available. Make one-on-one communication with an employee a priority. Only emergencies or vacations should infringe on those meetings. Set a schedule, and keep it.

▸ If you can't be at the meeting, have a contingency plan in place.

▸ Make sure the meeting is free from disruptions or distractions. (Close the office door; don't take incoming calls.)

▸ Have your notes available to review daily performance and commitments made during previous meetings.

▸ Insure that the meeting is a positive, partnering experience. The employee should feel that the meeting is a benefit, not a waste of time, or an audit or evaluation.

The way in which you conduct the one-on-one is crucial. Your goal is to build up, not beat up, the employee! Superstar leaders do the former and bad bosses the latter. Make it your goal to be helpful and to develop your employees, and not to be hurtful and immobilizing.

Remember the High-Performance Formula discussed earlier. People need coaching, not destructive critics. Superstar leaders coach others well and instill in them a desire to excel. Poor bosses are generally too critical, and create resentment and defensiveness in others; they don't even try to be good coaches.

ASK is a useful acronym for remembering the key elements of the one-on-one process:

A—Ask questions. In a one-on-one you want a dialogue, not a monologue.

S—Seek solutions. Engage employees in discussion about progress on their goals, developmental areas, or problems. Get their opinions and ideas first, and then add your own comments.

K—Keep plans and commitments. Take notes to document your discussion. Ask employees to do the same so you can review progress at future meetings and track mutually agreed-upon plans of action.

The following outline includes the steps and talking points for conducting a one-on-one meeting:

Step 1: Pre-meeting preparation. (Action plans, numbers, goals, etc.)

Step 2: Greeting. (Be positive; make some small talk; ensure privacy.)

Step 3: Ask employees to reconfirm their goals and to share their results and progress on their plans. Praise progress, recognize good performance, and identify areas to improve:

How did your day/week/month go?

What progress did you make on your goals and action plans?

What went well?

What didn't go well?

Step 4: Ask the employee to tell you how and why he or she made decisions:

What was your thinking process?

What did you do next?

What more could you have done?

What can you do differently or better next time?

How can you help more in the future?

Step 5: Seek solutions and build a new plan on how to improve the results:

What ideas do you have for improvement next time?

What do you think of this idea...?

Did you try...?

Are you open to some suggestions?

The benefit of this is....

Have you thought of about trying...?

This is what I recommend....

Step 6: Keep plans and commitments. Make sure to review all key action steps from the last meeting, and set new goals and action steps.

Step 7: Summarize your discussion and the action plan.

Step 8: Schedule another meeting and show your appreciation for the employee's efforts.

A one-on-one is specifically about effective communication. You talk about goals, expectations, problems, and solutions to those problems. You give employees positive feedback about their efforts while identifying performance issues clearly and directly. You develop employee skills and attitudes about getting the job done well and achieving the best results.

In one-on-ones, you train employees to think proactively when faced with challenges, obstacles, and problems. Through the course of time, the process teaches them problem-solving skills they can implement on their own. They become innovative and learn to take initiative to go the extra mile. The one-on-one process helps everyone explore ways to creatively improve performance, not merely get the job done. The payoff is really big if you execute coaching brilliantly. A study by Public Personnel Management compared training alone to daily performance management through coaching and training found that training alone increased productivity by 22.4 percent, and training plus coaching increased productivity by 88 percent.[1] Awesome!

Day 12 Superstar Leader Application
What did you learn from this section on coaching through one-on-ones?
What are your strengths in coaching?
In what areas can you improve?
How will you implement one-on-one meetings with your employees?

The task of the leader is to get his people from where they are to where they have not been.

—Henry Kissinger

Day 13
COACHING
IMPROVEMENT

Though we aren't big fans of using sports analogies in business applications, there are some valuable illustrations in the realm of sports.
A football coach was lauded as one of the best in the game after his team
won the Super Bowl. He was idolized for his tough talk, but he often belit-
tled his players and cussed up a storm. In the years that followed, his teams
struggled to have a winning season.

An infamous basketball coach with several NCAA titles consistently
received lauds and acclamation in spite of throwing chairs and pushing
players around. He won titles in the past, but even before retiring he
hadn't won in years in spite of the talent on his teams. If these behaviors
were applied regularly in business, there would be no commerce—everyone would be in court fighting lawsuits. Pat Riley, author of *The Winner
Within,* said, "A coach must keep everyone on the team in touch with
present-moment realities—knowing where they stand, knowing where
they're falling short of their potential, and knowing it openly and fairly."[1]

Effective coaching is a difference-maker in employee achievement.
Most managers are poor at coaching; they either yell or tell people what to
do to motivate them, or they simple bypass coaching because it takes time
and hard work. As you've been learning, both informal and formal coaching requires specific, continuous actions and processes to be successful.
Effective coaching touches on all the elements that Frederick Herzberg
talks about for employee motivation, as well as for the High-Performance
Formula. Coaching works!

One manager asked his 10 employees to rate him on his coaching skills
in a 360-degree confidential assessment. He thought he was a good coach.
Some of his employees agreed that he was a good coach, and others asked,
"What coaching?" He learned he was rubber-stamping his approach and
treating everyone the same, when in fact they had different strengths,
goals, and needs. He intentionally changed his methods and went on to
become an exceptional coach, achieving his best results ever.

If you want to be a good boss—maybe a Superstar boss—why wouldn't
you want to improve your coaching skills? Thoughtfully review the following coaching chart, and then rate yourself the way you think employees
might rate you, not as you might hope to be.

Best/Worst Boss and Coaching

DIRECTIONS: Circle the four to six behaviors in the "BEST BOSS BEHAVIORS" column that you do most of the time; put a checkmark by the behaviors that need improvement in the "WORST BOSS BEHAVIORS" column.

COACHING SKILLS	BEST BOSS BEHAVIORS	WORST BOSS BEHAVIORS
Communicates clear performance goals and expectations.	Sets specific goals. Explains what is expected. Clarifies expectations often. Reinforces goals/expectations.	☐ Sets vague, unclear, or ever-changing expectations. ☐ Sets general goals or none at all.
Meets regularly in one-on-ones for coaching.	Conducts informed and timely meetings. Provides generally positive feedback. Gives clear verbal feedback. Offers constructive feedback. Follows up.	☐ Provides incomplete or sporadic feedback. ☐ Misses meetings or fails to do one-on-ones. ☐ Requires employees to request help and feedback.
Asks for a summary of results and activities.	Creates a dialogue, not a monologue. Engages the employee through questions and problem-solving. Remains objective about the process. Recognizes progress and results.	☐ Is regularly critical and negative. ☐ Formulates preconceived ideas. ☐ Does most of the talking. ☐ Tells the employee what to do with limited or no input.
Sets plans and commitments.	Asks for input or improvement. Provides immediate feedback. Offers specific ideas or suggestions for improvement.	☐ Does little or no planning. ☐ Provides general feedback. ☐ Fails to offer constructive advice.
Keeps commitments and action plans.	Understands the strengths and weaknesses of individuals. Develops personal and professional relationships with employees. Holds self and others accountable for results through follow-up.	☐ Operates in a detached mode. ☐ Limits involvement in developing improvement plans.

COACHING SKILLS	BEST BOSS BEHAVIORS	WORST BOSS BEHAVIORS
Praises progress and recognizes positive results.	Gives public praise. Aggressively seeks rewards for employees. Recognizes work in difficult situations.	☐ Recognizes and praises infrequently or not at all. ☐ Selectively recognizes and rewards high performance.
Provides timely and regular feedback and guidance.	Focuses on employee strengths. Offers help and ideas. Encourages training. Gives personal advice.	☐ Is mostly critical in feedback. ☐ Is indifferent to or uninformed about employee strengths, weaknesses, and needs.
Makes the time to coach in one-on-ones and build positive relationships with high expectations.	Communicates well. Listens well. Genuinely offers help. Cares about employee success.	☐ Is uncomfortable with one-on-ones. ☐ Focuses on data, facts, electronic communication, and "administrivia."

Coaching for Excellence Inventory

DIRECTIONS: Rate yourself on the following in terms of how often you engage in the listed behavior. Use a scale of 1 to 5, with 5 being very frequently and 1 being rarely. Be honest and rate yourself the way you think employees might rate you, not as you might hope to be. When you're finished rating yourself, put a plus sign by the top five scores and a check mark by the lowest scores.

Review goals and expectations.	Rating	+/✔
1. I set aside uninterrupted and private time to meet with my employees individually. 2. I discuss agreed-upon goals/expectations with my employees. 3. I review employee goals/expectations at the start of each of our coaching sessions.		
ASK to gain employee perspective and input.		
4. I encourage open discussion when I hold coaching meetings. 5. I ASK for employee input when reviewing performance. 6. I listen and paraphrase what employees are trying to say. 7. I carefully assess all factors that affect employee performance results. 8. I regularly observe employees in action with customers or others.		
Provide feedback and guidance.		
9. I recognize and reward high performance. 10. I give regular/immediate feedback to employees in a constructive manner. 11. I listen to employee feedback and concerns before expressing my own. 12. I am specific about behaviors and tasks when I give advice or guidance. 13. I focus on using and reinforcing the strengths of employees. 14. I provide feedback that is appropriate to employee situations, performance level, and goals. 15. I teach new skills clearly and systematically.		
Develop action plans.		
16. I develop specific action plans to help improve employee skills/results. 17. I gradually give more responsibility to employees so they can grow. 18. I ensure that employees understand and agree to their action plans. 19. I hold people accountable for results. 20. I negotiate project tasks and deadlines with experienced people.		
Establish follow-up.		
21. I set up follow-up meetings at the conclusion of our coaching meetings. 22. I ensure that follow-up coaching meetings take place.		

Day 13 Superstar Leader Application
What are your strengths in coaching?
In what areas can you improve?
What is your plan to get started with superstar coaching?

All employees are motivated. It's the leader's job to inspire people.

—Rick Conlow

GIVING POSITIVE FEEDBACK AND REWARDS

DAY 14: Principles of Recognition

DAY 15: Informal Recognition

DAY 16: Formal Recognition

Day 14
PRINCIPLES OF RECOGNITION

What motivates people? If you recall our earlier discussions, recognition is a prime motivator. This is the positive side of giving feedback. People want to be noticed and valued for what they do. According to research, 91 percent of employees want more recognition at work, and only half say they get any at all.[1] Gallup's research found that employees who said they were recognized in the last week tended to perform better in the following week.[2] Contrast this with the fact that most managers don't realize that praised behavior is behavior that will be repeated; most managers think it is wrong to brag about an employee in front of others. A manager reported that after giving recognition to an employee, the employee cried. When asked why, she said, "I have worked here for 26 years, and you are the first person to give me recognition for my job." Though this may be an extreme case, it points out a blaring weakness in the leadership practices of many managers.

Ken Blanchard's work with Situational Leadership continually emphasizes that managers need to catch people doing things right and to comment on it—give them recognition.[3] There are several key principles to follow when giving both informal and formal recognition (which will be discussed at length in the following chapters):

- ▶ **Be genuine.** Give recognition from the heart because an employee deserves it, and it's the right thing to do to make employees feel valued and good about the job they do. Give recognition because you care. Don't give it falsely or because you want something.

- ▶ **Be specific.** Say, *"Josh, you did a great job listening to the customers' concerns and offering options for a solution. You made me proud to have you on my team,"* as opposed to simply saying, "Great job!" or "Super!" or "Way to go." Nobody knows what you are talking about, even though it might sound good. Give employees credit for what they have accomplished. They can see through phony comments.

▶ **Be personable.** Think in terms of employee needs. Some people prefer open verbal expressions, so praise them that way. Others like things more private, so give praise one-on-one. If you can give rewards, for example, provide a dinner to an employee's favorite restaurant or lift tickets to an employee who likes to ski.

▶ **Be immediate.** Give recognition as soon as possible. Saying thank you today to someone who worked late six weeks ago is unproductive. Saying thank you at the time the work is done is much more powerful.

▶ **Be public.** Take into consideration the employee's needs, and then be public. Tell others what happened. Offer praise in front of others; praise an employee at a meeting. Put the news in the departmental newsletter, or send out an e-mail.

▶ **Stay positive.** Recognize employees related to their achievement or progress on goals or projects, but don't turn around and criticize them for poorer performance on other projects/goals.

▶ **Recognize often.** Too often, mangers get busy and forget to recognize employees, and they forget (or don't know) the motivational value it provides. Pay attention, and notice the efforts people are putting into their jobs. Look for ways to compliment people on their efforts daily. You don't have to praise every little thing employees do; you do need to genuinely appreciate their efforts. They will respond with increased performance, and they will choose to go the extra mile.

▶ **Recognize those who recognize others.** In other words, compliment those who take the time to appreciate the work of others.

▶ **Be creative.** Change the ways in which you recognize people. An employee of the month award, for example, can be a valuable tool, but beware, lest it become a stale popularity contest month after month and the meaning of the reward get lost. Consider letting employees choose who gets the award, or give 10 awards instead of one. Change the criteria every month, or find another type of recognition. Have employees praise other employees at a staff meeting. There are many resources for recognition ideas, such as Bob Nelson's book *1001 Ways to Recognize Employees.*[4]

▸ **Be persistent.** Genuine recognition of employees will create a different work atmosphere, but it requires persistence. Stick with it, and try different approaches. Remember that you are recognizing employees because it matters. You are positively affecting someone's life, not merely motivating for performance. You can fan the flames of your employees' internal motivation to excel. They will feel more confident and important because of the recognition you give.

A Toronto service company we work with consistently performs better than its competition in service, sales, and profits. When you walk into the company's office, you sense a difference. Throughout the location, you see employee recognition: employee pictures on the walls; goals listed on white boards and bulletin boards; posted charts and graphs that show their current progress; and plaques, trophies, and certificates of their achievements adorn their meeting room. They have implemented Superstar strategies consistently and passionately.

Contrast that with a business in Minneapolis that posted an employee of the month picture in the entryway of the office. In December one year, you could see that the last employee award was from July. Not surprisingly, that office was in constant turmoil; the company had cameras videotaping employees while they worked to reduce theft problems.

Which place would you rather work? Which place would bring out the best in you? Managers who do not give positive recognition and praise typically have two big excuses: 1) They don't have time for it, and 2) they hire good people who "know what to do and don't need a babysitter." This is dinosaur thinking. Superstar leaders find the time for employee recognition; bad bosses don't. You find time for the things you believe in, but ultimately, employee recognition can be built into the fabric of your daily communication and leadership practices without taking extra time.

Superstar leaders know that appreciation is a cornerstone of good relationships. Recognition is the basis for giving medals at the Olympics, medals and ribbons in the military, and much more. People appreciate being appreciated, and recognition helps people develop a sense of pride in accomplishing worthwhile business goals.

Many managers excuse their lack of employee recognition by saying they don't know how to do it. They understand that showing appreciation can be helpful, but they become nearly mechanical in their attempts at recognition. In the next two days, we will review a multitude of ways to praise and reward in employees through informal and formal recognition.

Day 14 Superstar Leader Application
Think of time you were praised for a job well done. Why did you receive the recognition and how did it make you feel?
What principles of recognition have you tried to follow?
What are the obstacles to you doing more recognition and how can you overcome this?

One of the greatest compensations in life is when you help others, you help yourself.

—Samuel Smiles

Day 15
INFORMAL RECOGNITION

It's natural for the human spirit to desire praise, recognition, and appreciation. During an Excellence in Management workshop we do, we reviewed the concept of effective recognition and then gave the managers in attendance a "live action" assignment to go recognize two of their employees. At first, the managers resisted the idea because their employees weren't at the workshop. We listened to their concerns and brainstormed alternatives to face-to-face conversations (phone, text, fax, or e-mail). Each manager had to complete a form that stated who they contacted and how they gave recognition, and described the reaction of the employee. We even promised dessert of their choice at lunch if they completed the assignment! At lunchtime, the heartwarming stories of surprise and appreciation rolled in. The power of simple recognition was amazing.

Unfortunately, giving informal recognition seemed to be a challenge for many of the managers. We chuckle in recollection of one manager who needed extra coaching because he didn't quite get the concept. When we asked how the calls to his employees went, he responded, "Okay, I asked them, 'What great thing did you do for me today that I should recognize?'" He obviously still needed help with the concept. Many managers have some fair questions about the concept:

▸ When do you do it?

▸ How do you do it fairly?

▸ How often is appropriate?

▸ What if it doesn't work?

Informal recognition is a key ingredient to healthy relationships with employees. Regular and consistent informal recognition makes employees feel appreciated, respected, and valued. It involves praising them for progress on a goal, project, or other successful endeavor. Recall the principles of recognition we discussed earlier, and consider the following characteristics of informal recognition.

Informal recognition:

▸ Is a day-to-day activity.

▸ Has little or no cost.

- ▸ Focuses on specific behaviors, progress, or results.
- ▸ Builds positive and trusting relationships.
- ▸ Has immediate impact.

Here's an example: *"Good job, Sue! Thanks for taking the time to answer that customer's questions on the new product. That's what our customer intimacy process is all about. Your efforts made me proud to have you as part of our team."*

How long does it take to give such recognition? Only minutes. Of course, to give informal recognition, you have to be where your employees are, observing and listening. Look for ways to give everyone positive feedback and praise every week, if not more often. Informal recognition is not about looking over people's shoulders and saying, *"Good job!"* for everything they do. Informal recognition requires that you consistently let your employees know that you notice their good work.

Imagine the impact on employees if this became part of your regular management practices. How would employees feel? What kind of job would they do? Behavioral scientists say that praised behavior will be repeated. Superstar leaders learn to master informal recognition so that it is a seamless part of their day-to-day communication. Their employees and coworkers want to come to work; they do a good job because they feel good about it. Poor bosses struggle with recognition in any form; they are forever critical; they come across like politicians on the campaign trail looking for votes. Employees avoid those bosses, and they can't wait to go home at the end of the day.

Why should you informally recognize your employees? The reality of life is that people have problems, and they bring these problems to the workplace. Personal problems get added to work problems, and life stresses get them down. They need encouragement. Too often, they aren't getting it from others, so why not from you?

This kind of recognition is not effective if you only do it once in a while or if you only try it because you read this book. You have to genuinely care for people and realize that informal recognition isn't just about results but about the process as well. We spend a considerable number of hours at work. Why can't it be at least somewhat pleasant? Someone once said that this quote hangs over the entrance to Harvard Business School: "He who enters here will never smile again." Business may be serious, but people need to be appreciated. It's the right thing to do.

Following are some of the many ways to give informal recognition.

▶ Give verbal praise in a one-on-one coaching session.

▶ Give verbal praise in front of a few people.

▶ Give verbal praise in a meeting.

▶ Offer praise in a handwritten note.

▶ Offer praise in a thank-you card.

▶ Offer praise in an e-mail or a text message.

▶ Offer praise in an e-mail copied to others.

▶ Send a letter of commendation.

▶ Put the person's name in a company newsletter.

▶ Make a fun award in Microsoft Word and send it in a PDF file to the person.

▶ Praise a person who isn't present at the time, and have others pass on the recognition.

▶ Talk non-business to an employee.

▶ Delegate a new task and use good work on previous tasks as the reason.

▶ Take a person to lunch for progress on the job.

▶ Buy an employee a cup of coffee, glass of pop/soda, or a treat for reaching a milestone on a project.

▶ Make up a "good deed" card to recognize effort for improved customer service.

▶ Tell someone to go home early one day, especially if he or she is putting in extra effort.

▶ Give "high fives" to employees in a meeting after achieving a goal or completing a difficult action step.

▶ Decorate the office in honor of completing a project.

▶ Use an office bulletin board or company intranet dashboard to track results and give encouraging words for goal progress.

▶ Recognize others for giving recognition.

▶ Lend a helping hand on a difficult project or when crunched by a time line, and share appreciation to others who do likewise.

▶ Ask for input and give an example of how a person helped in the past.

▶ Get someone a balloon that says "thank you," and explain it later.

▶ Be creative. Try different things at different times. Don't get bogged down doing the same old things.

In all the recognition, it needs to have some common sense sprinkled in and be genuine, not done because "we need to praise people today." Many organizations are trying all kinds of activities to recognize, but often go overboard. For example, one company executive I talked with recently said one of his projects teams had a meeting. There were 17 people on the team. Ten received recognition for progress, and it took 30 minutes of the meeting. The seven who didn't get a pat on the back felt badly. The recognition had a negative connotation. To make matters worse, the team was behind on its time line. Recognize because it is deserved when significant progress is evident or the goal was achieved, not because someone showed up for work. Finally, it goes back to setting clear expectations, and ensuring your expectations are high, worthy of accolades, and of a Superstar leader.

Day 15 Superstar Leader Application
What did you learn or relearn about informal recognition?
List five to seven informal recognition methods will you commit to using.
Name two people you can recognize today and describe how you will do it.

Love 'em and lead 'em.

—General John Henry Stanford

Day 16
FORMAL RECOGNITION

To: All Employees

Subject: A special Thank You

Last week's record-breaking cold weather brought out the "true grit" in all of us. It was gratifying to see many employees helping customers and fellow employees with many problems resulting from the cold weather.

On Monday morning my desk was filled with employee "Good Deed" cards expressing appreciation for helping each other by fixing heaters, starting cars, plowing snow, giving rides, and working late to get customers' cars on the road.

Thanks for your pride in customer and employee satisfaction!

Dave

All of Dave's employees received a copy of this note, and Dave personally talked to many of them. Dave retired after a long career as an executive in a large automobile dealer organization. It is plain to see why his business was a leader in customer and employee satisfaction.

Although this could be an example of informal recognition, we show it in this section on formal recognition because it exemplifies the high-performance culture that Superstar leaders nurture.

Rick owns a tire franchise. The first part of his career he ran stores for the corporation. Every store he managed excelled and was among the most profitable stores in the company. Rick was put in a number of losing stores and turned them around in a year. The company wanted to promote him to the head office, but he didn't want to relocate, nor did he want to travel and be away from his family, so he bought a franchise.

Within a year of buying the store he was called to active duty for Operation Desert Storm. Whereas most small businesses would die with their owner gone for six months, his thrived. He set up a support network of professionals to help in his absence, but more than that, his employees stepped to the plate. Rick had invested in them so that when he needed their help most, they came through. Rick is truly a Superstar leader, and the results prove it.

The following are some of Rick's good boss management practices:

▶ Buy a birthday cake, and have a celebration for each new employee.

▶ Hold regular cookouts to celebrate employee success.

▶ Conduct goal-setting sessions for both job and personal goals.

▶ Hold ongoing meetings to focus on customer service.

▶ Provide cash bonuses beyond standard incentive pay for going the extra mile with customers.

▶ Help with financial problems or down payments on a house.

▶ Provide ongoing training.

▶ Treat all employees as professionals—no time clock needed.

When Rick first opened the store, he asked his team of 20 employees how they wanted to be treated—as professionals or as hired hands? He told them that pros come to work and do whatever it takes to care for customers on any given day, and they share in the profits. Hired hands punch in and punch out, get an hourly wage, and work by the clock. His employees unanimously agreed to be, and be treated as, professionals. Most brought their families to the store to tour their new business.

Methods such as these recognize the inherent pride people feel when they do well, achieve goals, and are part of something worthwhile.

Formal recognition:

▶ Costs money.

▶ Has specific criteria and results.

▶ Is given mostly to top performers.

▶ Spans significant time frames (week, month, quarter, year).

Here's an example: *"It's my pleasure, Jill, to present this customer satisfaction award to you for superior service ratings and teamwork! Thank you for your outstanding contributions."*

Many companies or managers don't use formal recognition because they have limited or no budgets. Public organizations often use that objection. It will take more creativity on a limited budget, but it is still possible.

Formal recognition needs to focus on the primary goals of the department and team. Without clear goals, it is difficult to do formal recognition. Bad bosses simply don't set goals, but Superstar leaders want top performance so they use every tool available to bring out the best in their employees.

Following are examples of formal recognition:

- Pay increase based on merit.
- Job promotions.
- Days off with pay.
- Certificates of achievement.
- Plaques for achievement.
- Trophies of achievement.
- Pins or ribbons for achievement.
- New job assignments.
- Exotic trips.
- Weekend getaways.
- Gift cards.
- Dinner or lunch certificates.
- Tickets to sporting events.
- Tickets to concerts or the theatre.
- Invitations to gala affairs or parties.
- Company logo t-shirts, caps, or jackets.
- Embroidered apparel that indicates the achievement.

Be creative. One company gives small teddy bears as service awards.

If you have little or no budget, use the informal recognition ideas with a bonus feature, such as the following:

▶ Chocolate or other candy (a great thank-you gift).

▶ Homemade certificates of achievement.

▶ Reserved parking space.

▶ Better office space.

▶ Verbal praise or applause in front of others.

▶ Letter of recommendation.

▶ Good deed cards.

▶ Boss for a day.

A growing medium-sized manufacturing company we worked with landed its biggest contract ever by agreeing to an aggressive time line and some up-front investment in equipment. To get the job done on time, the company needed employees to work overtime, but they didn't have the resources to pay them accordingly. Instead of threatening employees, management went to the employees and shared the problem.

Management opened the books about the financial challenges and opportunities with the particular customer. With team brainstorming and problem-solving, they arrived at a unique solution: The employees would do the overtime, and if they exceeded the deadline, they would get days off with pay from the money the company made by beating the deadlines. The plan worked, they improved productivity 25 percent to get the job done, and employees received their days off.

As we have discussed, Frederick Herzberg discusses recognition as a prime employee motivator. We believe more than 80 percent of performance problems are due to a lack of clear expectations/goals and a lack of proper recognition. People usually want to contribute and know that their work is noticed and valued by their employer.

Properly recognized people tend to perform exceptionally well. The Jackson ROI study showed that companies who recognize employees more have a greater return on their investment in the business. Authors Adrian Gostick and Chester Elton of *The Carrot Principle,* say that managers who do a better job of recognition:

▸ Have lower employee turnover rates.

▸ Achieve enhanced business results.

▸ Are seen as stronger in the basic management skills of goal setting, communication, trust, and accountability.[1]

Can you afford not to make recognition and praise a natural part of your leadership repertoire?

Day 16 Superstar Leader Application
What did you learn or relearn in this section?
What formal recognition methods will you use and why?
Which of your employees deserve formal recognition, and how will you recognize them?

The unexamined life is not worth living.

—Socrates

DELIVERING EFFECTIVE TRAINING

Day 17
TAKING TIME
TO TRAIN

Many bosses claim they don't have time to train. The better question is whether you have time not to train. If you provide ongoing learning opportunities for your employees, they will perform better. When they grow and learn, they are better able to try new things and make positive changes in their behavior because they have the confidence and ability to succeed. As we discussed earlier, this is a key component of employee motivation.

Fortune Magazine, as we have identified, annually selects the best hundred companies in the United States to work for. The company descriptions reveal a common characteristic: training. *Fortune*'s top-rated companies habitually provide 40, 50, 60, and 100-plus hours of training per year for all employees. We have already provided research to support the importance of ongoing training; here are a couple more:

▶ Forty-one percent of employees at companies with poor training plan to leave within a year, versus 12 percent of employees at companies with excellent training.[1]

▶ Companies that spend $273 per employee per year on training average 7-percent voluntary turnover compared with 16 percent for companies that average $218 per employee per year.[2]

As a manager, you don't have time not to train. Regular training is the key to employee effectiveness. Without it, other departments and other companies—your competition—will outperform you.

Managers also tend to excuse their non-training approach by saying, *"I am not a trainer."* Although that may be a fair assessment, training is a skill set that can be learned. If you are a manager who doesn't know how to train, you can begin the learning process now.

There are two areas to consider for training: the content and the process. In what areas do your employees need training (content), and how and by whom should that training be conducted (process)?

Content depends greatly on the type of job, but it can usually be defined by the technical and the interpersonal aspects (people skills). A sales rep needs technical training in product knowledge, paperwork, company procedures, and customer relationship management tools, as well as interpersonal training in consultative sales and customer service. A customer service rep needs similar training but with greater emphasis on the customer service skills. New hires need comprehensive training from A to Z. Experienced employees need training for new products, new software tools, policy changes, and refresher training on interpersonal skills. Ongoing reinforcement training is what separates the best from the rest. Too many companies and managers give all the training the first year on the job and then stop.

Reinforcement or supportive training helps people:

▸ Relearn what they forgot.

▸ Remind them of the proper way to do a skill.

▸ Focus on doing things the right way.

▸ Prevent bad habits from taking over.

▸ Learn from others and from their own mistakes.

▸ Share what they have leaned that may help others.

With good delivery and a little style, training becomes a positive force for increasing performance.

The process of training involves who does it, how to deliver it, and how to ensure it happens. We will focus in this chapter on who does it and how to get it done. (Day 18 focuses on the STAR process, and Day 19 focuses on training delivery.)

The process begins with you.

Your human resources (or personnel or training) department needs to be your training partner. If they are well funded and professional, they can help you design a training plan for your team. If they aren't, you will have to rely on your own team and outside resources. Obtain the answers to the following questions from your human resources (HR) department:

▸ Can they help you assess the training needs for new and experienced personnel on your team?

▸ In what areas can they help you?

▸ In what ways can they help you?

▸ How much time can they give you?

▸ What will it cost?

▸ When can they begin the process?

Except for some larger corporations, most HR departments are overworked, understaffed, and unprepared to meet all your needs. Get whatever assistance is available. The effort is important to you and your employees' success.

Outside vendors are another valuable resource for training assistance. Consider the following resources:

Training Publishing Companies

HRD Press and the American Society of Training and Development both have a mountain of training material for sales, teamwork, customer service, coaching, communication skills, and so forth, including leader's guides. Once you buy the materials, they are yours to tailor and deliver as needed. There are many on-line resources as well; ask for recommendations from your HR department and from other managers.

Smaller Local Colleges

Training at smaller colleges and technical schools is usually less expensive than their big-league counterparts, and the training they offer is usually good. Most of these schools have published business-training catalogs that list all their courses. They often have a training staff that will come to your site and teach courses. (Ask to audit one of their courses before paying for their on-site services to ensure their competence and their ability to meet your needs.)

Consultants

If your budget allows, hire a consultant to conduct training courses and work more closely with you. Ask sales, technology, or HR department or other managers for recommendations. (Again, be sure to interview the consultants, ask for and check on their clients, and ask to see them in action, too.)

The training process requires a strong training plan that includes the following steps: Determine technical and interpersonal training needs. Observe your people in action to learn their strengths and weaknesses, and take notes. Include resources in your training plan to help maximize their strengths and make improvements in the other areas. People are hired for their strengths, so build on them. Next, ask your employees what training they need. These two management actions—observation and questioning—will identify most of your training needs. Your HR department may also have assessment tools for your use.

Outline a plan for training new hires. This should include on-the-job training with regard to job duties, product knowledge, company information and resources, and department procedures and policies. Determine what other team members will help with the training. Put this plan in writing. Including a simple checklist is helpful. Keep a completed copy in the new employee's file.

Outline a plan for training other personnel. Focus on the job duties that are unique to the individual employees. For example, focus on the latest technology developments for your computer technician. Send supervisors to management training sessions at a local college. Plan training that relates to your company's products, software, financials, and so forth.

Use employees to provide on-the-job training (OJT) to others. New people need to learn (and relearn using new methods) the technical aspects of their jobs. Train supervisors or other qualified employees to do one-on-one OJT to ensure that tasks are done properly. (Simply telling an employee to do something does not ensure that the employee knows how to do it.) OJT can provide big dividends. Here is a simple but effective OJT process: 3P + E.

1. **Present it.** Demonstrate the task and explain the steps as you go along. Provide a written explanation as well. Demonstrate as often as necessary for the employee to understand.

2. **Practice it.** Let the employee practice. Provide feedback, especially encouragement and praise for right actions. Demonstrate again how to do anything that seems difficult for them to grasp.

3. **Perform it.** Let the employee perform independently for a short period of time.

4. **Evaluate it.** Review what was done right and what needs improvement. Be supportive and encouraging. Repeat the process if the employee needs further help or to demonstrate another new task.

In addition to training for your employees, you, as a manager, also need a training plan. Determine your strengths and areas you need to improve as a manager. Plan at least one two- or three-day training course per quarter for yourself, as well as for all your employees. We've known managers who have taken more than a hundred different training sessions in their 20-year management careers to improve their skills.

Some people say you train animals and educate people. The reality is that people train all the time. Athletes train. Boxers train. Musicians practice. Without training, they don't become the best in their field. The same applies to business professionals; they need additional training—education—too. They also need ongoing practice to improve on specific skills.

We aren't talking about a one-shot, one- to two-day training session; now it is done. For training to be effective, it needs to be ongoing and interrelated. Geoff Colvin says in his book *Talent Is Overrated* that the best performers deliberately practice significantly more than others to reach the top in their fields.[3] If we want our teams to be the best, they have to work at it and keep learning and practicing their professions.

In the business world, any company can replicate a competitor for the short term, but though a company can copy services, it cannot reproduce people. People are the true competitive edge, and what makes them competitive is how much smarter they are today than they were yesterday. A good boss will use a variety of resources to continually train employees and bring out their best.

Make your training plans today. Don't wait. Get into action.

In the next section (Day 18), you will learn about the STAR training process that provides an outline to help you with the actual training preparation and delivery.

Day 17 Superstar Leader Application
Directions: Based on what you have just learned, begin to outline a training plan for your team. This is a starting point; you will want to get input from others as well. Include the training essentials in this outline: what, how, when, and by whom.
Overall Training Needs
Training Needs for New Hires
Training Needs for Other Personnel
Your Own Training Needs

Knowledge must come through action; you can have no test which is not fanciful, save by trial.

—Sophocles

Day 18
THE STAR TRAINING PROCESS

The Disney organization gives their cast members (mostly 18- to 20-year-olds) more training in a few months than many professionals get in their entire career! Disney has world-class customer service and has the best theme parks in the world.

Athletes train incessantly to stay on top, and those who don't usually lose their competitions. A few years ago, golfer Tiger Woods got in a slump and didn't win many majors; he said it was because he didn't take enough practice swings. To be the best, you have to prepare the most. Brian Tracy, whom we heard speak at a motivational conference in Minneapolis and who is a master sales trainer, said this about training and education, "The will to win isn't everything; the will to *prepare* to win is everything."

To be successful in business, you have to prepare to succeed. To do that requires effective training. Consider the difference between education and training.

Education is predominantly:
- The transfer of knowledge.
- Didactic in nature.
- Subject-/content-centered.
- Filled with teacher-driven learning activities.
- For long-term application.

Training is primarily:
- The transfer of skills.
- Experiential in nature.
- Performance-focused.
- Filled with participant-driven learning activities.
- For immediate application.

Superstar leaders encourage their employees to further their education or obtain advanced degrees. They also provide every available training opportunity to help their employees learn and apply new skills, concepts, and ideas to do their daily jobs. As previously stated, growth and learning are key motivators. Give your people more opportunities to learn, and they will find new ways to excel.

Bad bosses don't take time for training, or, if they do, they want a comprehensive program in three hours for $99! Bad bosses typically don't want to be involved in the process. They believe it is an HR department concern.

Superstar leaders model the way, as James Kouzes and Barry Posner discuss, and keep learning all along.[1] Superstar leaders also do training; they don't wait for HR to show up with the training manual, and they don't delegate all learning to on-line courses. E-learning has its place to provide knowledge, but to learn to apply the knowledge, experiential practice and workplace applications are needed.

Superstar leaders know the value of training, and they take time to learn how to train effectively. Training does not require a big budget or a certified trainer, but it does require a good grasp of the fundamentals. Many training sessions are overloaded with boring one-way communication; the manager talks with too many PowerPoint slides, and the employees listen. Without involving employees in the process, getting feedback, and practicing skills, training doesn't actually take place. Employees need to discuss ideas and then put to work what they have learned. Our STAR method will help you conduct effective training sessions that get results.

The STAR training process is a simple, cost-effective way for managers to conduct hands-on training on their own. We have used it in a variety of industries and companies. We have taught managers through "train-the-trainer" sessions worldwide and know they can do it, if they get the training and support materials.

Leaders have the responsibility to mine every employee's potential through good training, coaching, and re-training. The STAR training process is a way for managers to accomplish that. The STAR method of training is experiential; it uses role-play, simulation, and other activities to practice skills that directly relate to employees' careers or current jobs. A STAR training session can teach new concepts and skills or strengthen old ones, and a session can be completed in 30–60 minutes. Because everyone is a potential star, the program is labeled with the STAR acronym:

> S—Start positively
> T—Train and Educate
> A—Activity
> R—Review

Managers can use this format to train employees in their specific area of business. The training session is designed to be short, so preparation is key. Think through the meeting flow, and prepare a handout based on the outline provided here. This format makes the meeting specific to your group's needs; it isn't the generic offering of a training company. Your biggest benefit is that you learn best what you have to teach. (For a variety of training tools and resources that any manager can use, immediately go to our Website, *www.wcwpartners.com*, and click on Online Store.)

Randy is a manager for a company in the Midwest. He used the STAR method of training. At first he was unsure about his ability to train, but with preparation, support, and experience he improved every time. In his first session, he essentially read his outline word-for-word, and he was reluctant to get people involved. Through time and with practice, he learned how to encourage role-playing, and he became more adept at teaching new skills. Today, Randy is an outstanding trainer who conducts regular and as-needed service and meetings with his team. His employees have set new standards for performance for four years in a row!

Training with excellence is based on a good communication process. We need to present good content and present it well. It takes preparation, but any manager can make the commitment and accomplish this objective. Although the most common objection from managers is lack of time, consider these questions:

▸ Do you have time for customer complaints?

▸ Do you have time to fix errors?

▸ Do you have time to replace someone who quit or was fired?

▸ Do you have time to better serve customers?

▸ Do you have time to do a quality job?

▸ Do you have time for better performance from your employees?

Training may not seem to be an urgent need, but it is an investment in service, quality, productivity, and employee retention. Superstar leaders have time for that. Less-effective leaders do not. Which are you?

The following outline is an example of a STAR training session. The italicized words are those that would change with the subject matter. This example relates to customer service.

Star Training Topic: Handling Complaints
Start Positively (5 minutes)
Be enthusiastic. Review your department's service goals and the goal of the meeting.
Review *customer survey* results and give recognition.
Train and Educate (5–10 minutes)
Distribute and discuss prepared handout. *In this example, the handout lists five to seven common complaints from customers; ask the group for others. Discuss and share ideas on how to handle complaints. A second handout lists your recommendations or procedures. (The handouts are not included here.)*
List key points on a flipchart.
Activity (10–15 minutes)
Role-play. *For example, get employees involved by role-playing how to handle one of two complaints.*
Demonstrate proper or alternative methods.
Discuss what was learned; ask questions.
Review (5 minutes)
Summarize key points and compliment contributors.
Offer a contest or incentive for improvement. Praise several more people for good results.
Set up post-training coaching to review and evaluate application. *All training needs reinforcement lest people return to old habits. Example of follow-up in this case: listening to the reps as they make customer service calls and giving them feedback, conducting one-on-ones with reps to review their results, or informal coaching and interacting with reps.*

Day 18 Superstar Leader Application
Directions: Create your own STAR training session. Fill in the blanks to prepare your outline.
STAR Training Topic:
Start Positively (5 minutes)
Be enthusiastic. Review your department's [*list*] goals and the goal of the meeting.
Review [*list*] results and give recognition.
Train and Educate (5–10 minutes)
Distribute and discuss prepared handout.
List key points on a flipchart.
Activity (10–15 minutes)
Role-play.
Demonstrate proper or alternative methods.
Discuss what was learned; ask questions.
Review (5 minutes)
Summarize key points and compliment contributors.
Offer a contest or incentive for improvement.
Set up post-training coaching.

I hated every minute of training, but I said, 'Don't quit. Suffer now and live the rest of your life as a champion.'

—Muhammad Ali

Day 19
TRAINING
PRINCIPLES

Training is not an easy task. To be an effective trainer, you need to know how adults learn and how to fully engage them in the training process. People learn best by doing, not by hearing alone. Your efforts will be most effective and profitable if you focus on some basic principles. It's also hard work because to gain the benefit, you have to keep at it. That's what separates the best from the rest.

Setting the Stage

The first few minutes of a training session are crucial. If the opening is interesting, informative, and pleasant, you'll get people excited about the meeting. If it is boring, pointless, and unpleasant, you'll lose them for the duration. Make the training environment as pleasant as possible.

▸ Select a room that is neither too crowded nor too spacious.

▸ Seek decor that is pleasing to the eye. (Bright colors are best.)

▸ Make the room physically comfortable. (Check the thermostat.)

▸ Choose chairs that are large enough and soft enough.

The psychological atmosphere should be one of mutual respect. Be supportive and caring. Share your feelings. Be warm and friendly. Seek collaboration, not competition. Invite people to share what they know and can do. Speak and act openly and honestly. Focus on the needs of your employees to help them relax, and minimize any nervousness or apprehension.

Begin your training session with four basic steps.

1. Greet participants warmly and enthusiastically. Help them get comfortable. Thank them for being on time and part of the training.

2. Spell out the ground rules and protocol for the program. This includes things like responsibility, participation, breaks, agenda, and sensitivity to others.

3. Do an activity (an icebreaker) to get people acquainted.

4. Explain the goals of the training session.

By following these four basic steps, you can be sure that the stage is properly set and your trainees are ready to learn.

Learning by Doing

Calvin Coolidge said, "All growth depends on activity." Your employees will learn if they get involved in the process. We discussed the importance of this with the STAR method. Small groups, role-playing, assessment, case studies, simulations, and structured activities are the most valuable. It is important for people to participate in the activity, review or discuss it, and then apply what they have learned.

For example, instead of talking about communication, practice listening skills. Instead of talking about selling, role-play sales calls. Instead of talking about recruiting, brainstorm ways to recruit more people. Instead of listing problems, brainstorm solutions. Instead of listening to another speaker, break into small groups and discuss ways to generate business. Remember the ancient Chinese proverb "I do, I understand."

Delivering With Style

The style of delivery in training sessions is also important. It is leadership by example because what you do speaks more clearly than what you say. The first step to good delivery is to be yourself. Ralph Waldo Emerson declared, "Insist on yourself; never imitate." Your delivery will be effective if it's uniquely yours. Your personal strengths can make you a successful trainer. Be effective in your own way.

Completing the Cycle

With or without a strong delivery, training is of little value if it does not meet employee needs. Training helps employees perform better for greater achievement. Help your employees discover what they need for ongoing learning, and deliver that need. Whether the needs encompass values, attitudes, skills, or knowledge, you'll miss the target if you aim in the wrong direction. Although people may be enchanted by your delivery, it won't help them if you miss the mark. Know their needs, and hit your target.

Ask yourself the following questions as you prepare your training session:

- What are the needs of my employees?
- Which needs can I meet or turn into training goals?
- What type of training program helps me meet those needs?
- When, where, and with what materials will I do the training?
- How will I evaluate the training and future training needs?

Training that is not carefully planned and prepared is like wandering through a maze with no destination in sight. Don't make the common mistake of scheduling a training session simply because "it's been a while" since your last one. Get to know your employees and their needs, and then plan training accordingly. You can discuss training needs during your regular business meetings, too. Better yet, do training in those meetings.

Develop a yearly training plan for your area of responsibility. Schedule programs on a regular basis, not with a hit-or-miss approach. Design new programs or use packaged programs to meet your employee needs. Work with others, and draw upon their ideas and strengths in planning and conducting training programs.

Consistently training employees provides them the opportunity to improve. Improvement creates excitement that generates more business. When you train in a strong, focused, and well-planned manner, you will see improved performance. You have seen the studies that predict better productivity as a result of your efforts. Why not experience it for yourself?

To summarize, determine needs, set goals, develop designs, organize materials, deliver training, and evaluate results. Complete this cycle, and you'll produce successful training sessions and outcomes for your business.

Day 19 Superstar Leader Application

NOTE: Most managers aren't good trainers. They need more information. See the material that follows on training methods and adult learning.

Training Methods That Work

The following methods have proven successful for business training. Include a variety of methods when planning effective training sessions. Circle 3–4 of the items below that you have used to train others. Highlight two you want to learn more about, and go to the Web and seek out some examples. (Add these to your action plan at the end of the book.) See our book *The New Field book for Training* for other ideas. (It's on our online store at *wcwpartners.com.*)

1. **Role-Playing.** Two or more people act out a situation (customer and salesperson, for example) to practice a skill such as handling complaints. Observation and constructive feedback are necessary to reinforce the skill.

2. **Discussion.** Two or more people discuss their reactions to several questions and report their results to the group. Good listening and positive reinforcement are key elements.

3. **Flipchart/Chalkboard/White Board.** List key concepts for everyone to see, and refer to them during the presentation. This reinforces the learning process and stimulated recollection.

4. **Presentation.** Identify key skills or highlight important information. This reinforces ideas learned or practiced and sets a tone for learning.

5. **Simulation.** An activity or game that focuses on the content and process of a concept to raise awareness of how a concept influences the people involved. The trainer needs to observe and discuss how the simulation plays out.

6. **Question-and-Answer Session.** Use at the end of a simulation or meeting to deal with concerns, problems, or other ideas. Q&A validates knowledge and addresses problems.

7. **Reports.** Use after discussion to give participants a chance to share their ideas or feelings.

8. **Recap.** Use at the end of a meeting to highlight or summarize the most important points. This serves as reinforcement for learning.

9. **Testimonies.** Allow one or two people to share their expertise before the group. Testimonials add to the practical nature of the training and validate the expertise of others.

10. **Brainstorming.** Use in a group to generate ideas. All ideas are acceptable; don't eliminate or criticize any ideas. List all ideas on a flipchart, white board, or chalkboard for all to see. This method gives everyone a chance to participate and maximizes everyone's contributions.
11. **Videos/DVDs.** Use to reinforce content either as an introduction or a recap to add variety and visual effect. Using a video/DVD as the primary focus of a meeting is not effective without additional discussion or learning activities.[1]

Understanding Adult Learners

The most effective training occurs when trainers understand how adults learn. Consider these important principles. Check 3–4 of these principles that make the most sense to you and add them to your action plan at the end of the book.

☐	**Daily Application.** People want to learn what they can use in the present. Ideas, techniques, and methods must be practical, not theoretical.
☐	**Experience-Based.** People have experience and knowledge that is useful. Good training or coaching relates to what they already know and uses it to implement new solutions or to solve current problems. Ask for and use employee ideas or comments to acknowledge their experience and progress.
☐	**Professional Approach.** Effective training or coaching is a step-by-step process that people can understand and follow. With proper preparation and materials, training helps people learn and improve. Unplanned training is poor training.
☐	**Doing vs. Listening.** People learn best by getting involved. The old saying is true: "Give a man a fish, and he eats for a day; teach him to fish, and he eats for a lifetime." Participation is far more beneficial than lectures.
☐	**Attention Span.** Most adults need focused training that moves quickly but systematically. Use short sequences of technique (10–15 minutes) before changing gears, and limit content sections to about an hour. One-on-one coaching similarly does not need to be longer than 30–60 minutes.
☐	**People Are Different.** Everyone learns in different ways and at different speeds. Use a variety of methods to accommodate these differences and to keep learning interesting.

☐ **Reinforcement.** To be effective, training must be ongoing, reinforced daily, and followed up or supported through coaching. Repetition is the mother of learning.
☐ **Positive vs. Negative.** A training meeting is not the place to criticize or ridicule others. Keep the meetings positive. Use people's names. Give recognition and compliments when they're due. No one is motivated to increase performance through screaming, swearing, or shaming. Positive reinforcement increases confidence and success.
☐ **Feedback.** To maximize the effect of training or coaching, managers must observe people in action, give credit for success, and correct poor performance.
☐ **Fun vs. Boring.** The more fun you have, the better. Training that is relevant and action-oriented can be fun and will motivate people to learn. Boredom fuels boredom.

It's not enough that we do our best; sometimes we have to do what's required.

—Sir Winston Churchill

LEADING WITH FLEXIBILITY

DAY 20: The Philosophy

DAY 21: The Practice: Managing With Flexibility

Day 20
THE PHILOSOPHY

Ken Blanchard, Paul Hershey, and Daniel Goleman have provided great help and insight into management flexibility. Blanchard and Hershey pioneered the concept of Situational Leadership based on the Ohio University and Michigan University studies that focus on the developmental level of employees and style of leadership that will help them be most successful. Employees are defined in terms of their competence (knowledge, skill) and commitment (motivation, desire). Based on these definitions, four leadership styles emerge: directing, coaching, supporting, delegating.

Goleman takes a broader organizational view of management flexibility and focuses on what an executive can do to best help the company. In his book *Primal Leadership,* he outlines six styles and their appropriate use:[1]

1. **Visionary.** Setting a new vision or direction.
2. **Coaching.** Helping employees improve long-term performance.
3. **Affiliative.** Healing rifts within teams during stressful times.
4. **Democratic.** Building consensus to gain employee input.
5. **Pacesetting.** Gaining higher quality results through a well-performing team.
6. **Commanding.** Dealing with a crisis or turnaround situation.

In our consulting experience, which is broad-based, practical, and extensive, we have determined three factors that drive leadership flexibility more than all others:

1. **Performance.** Are employees exceeding goals, meeting goals, or performing poorly? Are employees addressing job priorities?
2. **Priorities.** What are the employees' most important daily tasks, and are they getting done? How well are those tasks being performed?

3. **Person.** Do employees understand the priorities? How do the employees' strengths and weaknesses rate in their performance relative to these priorities? Do the employees have the skills or will to do the job effectively? Are employees being team players and customer-centered?

We have seen these factors played out in the trenches by department managers, sales managers, service or plant managers, and information services managers—the leaders who implement company strategies every day.

The answers to the questions posed by these factors create a variety of variables. Based on the answers to those questions, a Superstar leader must implement a full range of strategies to develop high-performing employees and teams, as pictured in the Superstar Leadership Model.

Understanding different strategies and adapting them to the needs of your employees or team is critical to helping them become more effective and productive. We call it "leading with flexibility," and it is one critical ingredient to the Superstar Leadership Model. These nine strategies comprise the Superstar leader's toolkit.

Superstar Leadership Model

How to Revolutionize Performance

Day 20 Superstar Leader Application
Think of two of the best bosses you have had.   How did they supervise you?
First:
Second:
What did they do that was similar?
What was different?
What can you learn from their approaches?

I long to accomplish a great and noble task, but it is my chief duty to accomplish small tasks as if they were great and noble.

—Helen Keller

DAY 21
THE PRACTICE: MANAGING WITH FLEXIBILITY

In the 1940s, Ohio State University and the University of Michigan each carried out independent studies in the area of leadership. The two universities identified leadership styles as combinations of "job centered and employee centered" behavior (Michigan) or "Initiating Structure Behavior and Consideration Behavior" (Ohio). The research found that job-centered managers are very directive; they watch subordinates closely, and use more formal communication patterns. Employee-centered managers create group cohesion, higher job satisfaction, and a friendlier working atmosphere.

The results of these studies launched subsequent development in leadership practices that have come to be known as "Situational Leadership." Hersey and Blanchard, Tannenbaum and Schmidt, Blake and Mouton, Rensis Likert, and many others have based some of their work on the fundamental outcomes of these groundbreaking studies.[1]

Superstar Leaders Vary Their Leadership Behaviors to Meet the Needs of Their Followers

Our experience and research in leadership effectiveness supports the idea that Superstar leaders are able to vary their leadership to meet a variety of needs experienced by different individuals who are involved in different tasks. (They are flexible leaders.) It is simple enough on its face to understand.

An individual who is less skilled in a specific task will do better with a significant amount of leadership guidance and direction related to the successful accomplishment of that task. And, when our follower is "steeped in" the behavior, knowledge, and experience required for successful performance of the task, he or she will need much less structure and guidance. Likewise, when an individual is enthusiastic and positively motivated to do a task, it follows that the individual will need less external encouragement and support than one who lacks confidence and enthusiasm for the task.

Superstar Leaders Are Customer-Centered

We (WCW Partners) also believe that Superstar leaders are customer-centered and that their followers are like their customers. Effective leadership is rooted in a two-way relationship, meaning that leaders (and good bosses) need to know their followers and let their followers know them.

What do we mean by that? Superstar leaders ensure that they know their followers' skill sets, work preferences, interests, values, and motivations. They also ensure that their followers know their (the leaders') values, standards of performance excellence, vision for the future, and specific performance goals. Communication and the investment of time are essential for the development and maintenance of these critical relationships.

A Word About Bad Bosses

Today's fast-paced, rapidly changing, and highly demanding work environment constantly challenges us in ways that can easily drive us toward behaviors associated with bad bosses. In our hearts, most of us believe that we are compassionate, understanding, results-oriented, and reasonable bosses. In reality, most of us are "working bosses," meaning that we are expected to not only lead others, but we maintain a hefty project list as high-level individual contributors as well. We are expected to participate in a never-ending schedule of meetings, and we receive a huge number of e-mails, voice mails, and text messages. As a result of this overwhelming workload and heavy pressure to perform, we may fall back on behaviors that are understandable but cause us difficulty.

Habitual Behavior—relying on behaviors that are old habits. In other words, we believe that this behavior is driven by habits rather than being well-thought-out, customer-centered (follower-centered) behavior. A common knee-jerk behavior is to do it yourself because it's easier than trying to tell or teach someone else to do it.

Expedient Behavior—doing what is "easiest for me at the moment" (rather than what's most needed). Often, this takes the form of a quick answer or decision that gets it off my plate—at least for the time being. A common example in a broad sense is that new managers often prioritize their individual contributor role in front of their employee/follower supervision and support. It takes time to meet, renew expectations, support problem solving, coach, and so on. It often feels expedient to bad bosses to invest this time in doing rather than leading.

In an early meeting with a new division president with a $500-million packaging company, one of our coaching clients made it clear that he really only wanted to work with people who were capable of identifying their own barriers to success and able to solve those problems for themselves. We also observed that when he did engage his "team members" in discussions, he had a tendency to bark directives—and to do so with a tone that communicated his impatience with them and his contempt for the intrusion they represented in his preferred work.

Needless to say, he was not loved or even respected by his followers. They avoided these painful discussions as frequently as they were able and participated reluctantly when avoidance was not an option. He was not a customer-centered manager, and he did not believe in spending time to establish an environment that supported excellence.

Many bad boss behaviors are easily characterized by some of the old folk sayings that have been around for years and persist as legitimate actions to take today. One that seems to show up more often than others is: "Throw them in, and see if they can swim." The results are almost always below expectations, and the employee or employees that are involved are not happy.

Superstar Bosses Stop to Think

The antidote is to take a moment to think. Then use the outcome of your thinking to act in a more successful and productive way. Think about what? First and foremost, think about the people you're leading and the needs they have to be successful.

As lifelong downhill skiers, we frequently see thoughtless behavior in action. Usually, it is an experienced amateur skier who enthusiastically puts his inexperienced friend on a ski lift and proceeds to the top of the mountain. After the pileup coming off the lift, the more experienced skier points his or her friend downhill, and with a great deal of confidence and assurance that everything will be fine, nudges him or her down the fall line.

Now, if you are a skier, you know the result. If you're not a skier, let us tell you that the results are usually not very pretty. First, it is very dangerous to the incompetent skier, and it is equally dangerous to everyone else on the chosen ski run. Usually, the skier has a miserable time, is terrified for his or her life and safety, gains no new competence, and frequently refuses to ski anymore. Sometimes you see these skiers angrily shuffling down the mountain (or sliding down on their behind), carrying their skis and poles because, even though it's a miserable way to get down, they believe their chances of getting down in one piece are much better than continuing on skis.

It is so much more effective (and appropriate) to provide appropriate training, guide them to appropriate terrain, closely coach them along, and to build on their success. Superstar leaders know this and ensure that they give tasks that are appropriate to their employees' abilities. They also calibrate the amount and frequency of task-specific direction, coaching, and support they provide to match the needs of their employees.

Shaping Your Leadership to the Needs of Your Followers

Your ability to lead your followers to successful outcomes begins and rests upon your ability to set and communicate clear expectations. You must know what results and outcomes you want and expect. It is also essential that you consider whether you've been there before or if you're charting new territory. If you've been there before, it's easier to zero in on the appropriate skills, behaviors, and procedures needed to produce the success outcomes you want. Training and coaching also rest on the knowledge and history developed previously.

If you haven't been there before, it requires you to decide what you want. What will success look like? In this case, you must "clear a pathway" to the result you want. Then, you'll need to master the skills and behaviors needed to produce excellence. It is both more difficult and more risky—leading while you learn. Often more communication, with a higher degree of structure, is required. This means task-focused, specific, outcome-based, and results-focused objectives with clear standards. How much? How many? And by when?

It's useful to identify where your followers are in order to choose the best way to meet their needs. (Head's up!—this is the "thinking part.")

Follower Skill Descriptions

Consider where followers are in terms of their skill, knowledge, and ability required for this specific task.

Beginner— Level I	This describes a person who has begun a course of instruction or is learning the fundamentals of the task. He or she has never been involved in this activity or task before. He or she is frequently unaware of the skills required and the risks associated with the task, and views it through a lens that is created by his or her (often) overly positive mindset about it.
Novice— Level II	A novice is new to a field or activity. He or she is beginning to learn to perform simple elements of the task in low-risk, low-pressure situations. He or she is more in touch with the realities of the task and has less-idealized views of what goes into it and what he or she will get out of it. The honeymoon is over.
Intermediate— Level III	An intermediate has learned the task and can perform in many or most circumstances. This individual frequently relies on models to guide him or her to success, and he or she performs well in low- to medium-risk and complexity. He or she may struggle with variable confidence levels and enthusiasm for the job.
Expert— Level IV	An expert has internalized and mastered the skill. This person can perform in complex and higher risk circumstances. He or she is equipped to handle the task in a variety of reality-based situations, and has a strong and clear set of internal standards about what is acceptable and what excellent performance looks like.

Hersey and Blanchard made the connection between the need for different styles (Ohio and Michigan Leadership Studies) and the needs of the follower. Their respective Situational Leadership models rest on the theory that different amounts (frequency of use) of direction and support make up the four different leadership styles they subscribe to and attempt to train their clients to utilize.

We also believe that Superstar leaders need to provide different amounts of task and personal guidance and attention to accommodate the skill, experience, and knowledge of the follower. So, in our previous ski example, a beginner on the ski slopes needs different type of ski instruction than an intermediate or expert. He or she also needs different guidance and consideration related to the type of terrain, equipment, and obstacles present. In the following table, you'll find a suggested leadership approach to address the capabilities and needs of each level of performance previously described. The Leader Approach points out/toward the kind of leader behaviors that are appropriate to the level of performance described at each level. The descriptions are not exhaustive and certainly require more complete and well-rounded leader behaviors than those highlighted here.

Skill Level	Description	Leader Approach
Beginner—Level I	A person who has begun a course of instruction or is learning the fundamentals of the task. He or she has never been involved in this activity or task before. He or she is frequently unaware of the skills required and the risks associated with the task, and views it through a lens that is created by his or her (often) overly positive mindset about it	Instructor and Guide—Provides the right orientation to the task, the terrain, the tools, the risks, and the obstacles. Introduces appropriate beginning tasks and opportunities to familiarize and practice. Carves out boundaries for safety and protects learner from extreme risk.
Novice—Level II	A person new to a field or activity. He or she is beginning to learn to perform simple elements of the task in low-risk, low-pressure situations. He or she is more in touch with the realities of the task, and has less-idealized views of what goes into it and what he or she will get out of it. The honeymoon is over.	Coach and Navigator—Provides exposure to the realities of the challenge, introduces scenarios that must be learned, calibrates practice opportunities appropriate to skill level, maintains boundaries for safety purposes, and increases complexity as knowledge and skill levels warrant.
Intermediate—Level III	An intermediate has learned the task and can perform in many or most circumstances. This individual frequently relies on models to guide him or her to success, and he or she performs well in low- to medium-risk and complexity. He or she may struggle with variable confidence levels and enthusiasm for the job.	Facilitator and Model—Models increasing levels of complexity as skill and perspective warrant. Facilitates practice that pushes skill and knowledge application. Provides distinctions necessary for the intermediate performer to gain perspective on his or her skill level and development needs.
Expert—Level IV	An expert has internalized and mastered the skill. He or she can perform in complex and higher risk circumstances. He or she is equipped to handle the task in a variety of reality-based situations, and has a strong and clear set of internal standards about what is acceptable and what is excellent performance.	Visionary, Strategist, and Supporter—Engages the follower in deeper and broader application of skill/ knowledge. Supports higher and deeper exploration and demonstration of skill, knowledge, and ability. Focuses on appropriate recognition of the expert's capability and contributions.

If you think about the development of one skill set from the beginner level through mastery, it is easy to see that the follower has different needs as he or she progresses through different levels of expertise. It requires that the good boss stay connected to the follower and his or her current skill level in order to adapt the leader's guidance and encouragement to the current level of the employee's capability. It is also important to remember that we all learn differently and at a different pace.

Day 21 Superstar Leader Application
Identify the skill levels of each of your employees on the main tasks they perform.
Based on the skill levels of your employees, identify the appropriate amount of guidance needed to help them succeed.
Consider past leadership situations in which you may have been less effective than you wanted. Is there a pattern to the misses that can provide guidance for your future leadership challenges? In other words, did you provide too much direction, too little direction, or some other identifiable mismatch that can inform you in the future?
What did you do, and what should you do in the future to be more effective?

People are definitely a company's greatest asset. It doesn't make any difference whether the product is cars or cosmetics. A company is only as good as the people it keeps.

—Mary Kay Ash

CREATING INCENTIVES AND FUN

Day 22
PRINCIPLES OF
INCENTIVES

Business is such serious stuff, it can be boring. People often come to work because they have to in order to receive a paycheck, not because they really want to.

There is a search for oil all over the world. In Canada, the economy is healthier than in many countries. The oil shale in the country is abundant and, with the price of oil, the business is growing. People from all over the country and world are flocking to the oil fields to make a living. The provinces without oil are hurting for workers because of this. Yet the living conditions by the oil fields are appalling. The companies are trying to make things all right with better temporary living quarters. Employees work 12–14 hours of the day, month in and month out. Some work for six months, go home for a month, and then return to work for six months.

Employees put up with this because the pay is good—better than most can get elsewhere. This seems to be a tough way to earn a living and live a life. The jobs with the oil companies are hard, dirty, unhealthy, and under harsh weather conditions.

Are the employees in the oil fields of Canada or other similar situations motivated to do this because of the company's efforts? Of course not. They endure this to make as much money as they can for themselves and their families. Yet how productive do you think they really are? Do they go the extra mile for the company? In reality, most do their jobs well, but few go the extra mile.

Do you think these employees could do better work? What if the companies created a whole new work environment and provided work-related incentives and activities that would more positively affect productivity, innovation, and safety? Times are changing, and managers all over the world are being called to step up their game, even on the oil fields of Canada.

One day while in Calgary on a consulting assignment we were having breakfast at the hotel. We noticed the two men next us. We overheard some of their conversations. They worked on the oil fields. The region manager was coaching the manager of local crews. They talked about production and safety. Hiring and the selection process came up, as a few crews were short workers. The discussion reviewed some of the men on the crews and their challenges or problems. The region manager did a good job of asking questions and listening while offering advice. Near the end of the conversation the region manager asked about morale and teamwork. His comments surprised us, but we certainly were impressed and pleased.

In the next two days, we will consider how to create a dynamic workplace through incentives.

Incentives are a way to highlight key company or departmental goals and challenge employees to be more effective. There are those who consider incentives just a way to make people work harder, but we look at incentives differently. Superstar leader strategies create work environments where employees like what they do and they already work hard. Incentives serve three other purposes:

1. **To challenge employees.** During sports playoffs, the players seem to raise their games to a new level. Why? Because victory—becoming the best—is a motivator.

2. **To recognize employees.** People like recognition. We need to do it even more. They will rise to the occasion.

3. **To have fun or more enjoyment.** Incentives give you a chance to change the pace of the job. Too many jobs become routine and repetitious. People become creatures of habit, and the result is mediocrity. By giving people a target to run for, it brings out their creativity and inner drive to succeed.

How Do You Set Up Incentives?

First, pick a business priority on which to focus. For example, the focus could be safety, productivity, idea generation, sales, service, customer service, quality, or profit. Identify the current performance level, and set a goal for improved performance. Use the SMART goal process to guide your decision-making.

Second, get input about the goal from your team. Brainstorm ideas with them, and try to find a creative way to implement your initiative. Be as creative as possible. Don't just show a safety video and announce that a reduction in incidents over the next month will earn everyone free pizza! Be more ingenious. Pick a theme, and have fun with it. Your employees will have ideas; use them.

After attending our leadership program, a manager in a Minneapolis business applied the Superstar Leadership Model strategies with her team of 40 direct reports. First, she assigned team leads to give people more attention. Then, she set goals, divided employees into teams, did cross-training, set up tracking charts, and promised to buy them lunch if they reached their goals and improved productivity. She achieved great success over a number of months but discovered one problem: Her employees were getting tired of pizza for a reward. (She was on a limited budget.) We suggested that she buy Subway sandwiches instead. She did and had even more success follow!

The following are examples of the names of sales and service incentives that have proven successful. In each case, the managers set goals for accomplishment, a time line, and created prizes to win individually. The prizes ranged from cash awards, to exotic trips, to the latest electronic gadgets.

- The Challenge.
- Poker Contest.
- Spin the Wheel.
- Five-Card Draw.
- Las Vegas Night.
- Deal or No Deal Event.

- Super Bowl Championship.
- World Series Challenge.
- The Stanley Cup Playoffs.
- Jeopardy.
- Valentine Love-King or -Queen.
- Holiday Awards.

As you consider these ideas, you can conjure up new ideas or ways to make them work for you. Companies who have used these ideas also decorated the workplace in keeping with the theme: posters, pictures, balloons, stars, crepe paper, ribbons, confetti, and charts/graphs. Employees may walk into a room with all of this and think they are at a birthday party, but the reality is that their workplace is transformed from plain and potentially boring to fun! Incentives generate interest and electrify the work climate.

When creating incentive plans, consider these important aspects as well:

Give everyone a chance to win. Any promotion can be team-based and individually focused. Regardless, some teams or people will always do better than others. If you only reward the top performers, you can be sure of the following goal-busters:

Some teams or people will give up.

Animosity, ill will, and jealousy will develop.

The fun is gone.

Yes, award the best performers, but set a goal for success where all participants can be rewarded. Focus on improved performance; too often, one team or person wins, and everyone else loses. Set a standard of performance, and give a reward to everyone who achieves it.

Keep it positive. Accentuate progress, improvement, and great performance throughout the event. At the conclusion of the program, recognize progress and improvement first, and then reward those who reached the standard. Finally, award the top performers. Don't chastise, ridicule, or criticize those who performed poorly or less than others. Don't give booby joke prizes (for example, winners get a fancy steak dinner and the losers get hotdogs and beans). Keep the sarcasm and snide remarks out of it, too.

Choose your rewards thoughtfully. Everyone is motivated by different things, so think outside the box. Use a variety of award possibilities through time. However, money, trips, and electronics are often the most popular payouts. Consider:

Brainstorming with your team, and use some of their ideas for prizes.

Personalizing the reward. One manager asked each customer service rep to name their prize if they reached a new level of service. He posted their choices, and after each meeting, they were given the option of applying their latest results to their personal long-term reward or taking a smaller monthly award.

Keeping your personal interests out of it. Not everyone likes baseball just because you do; nor does everyone enjoy golfing, fishing, or skiing.

Using certificates, plaques, and trophies. Though you need some of the payouts described here, people like the lasting recognition that these awards provide. Don't be cheap with this. Make sure the rewards are quality products.

Include a "wow" factor. When you ask for higher performance and effort, it is critical that big gains are rewarded with an exclamation point! For short-term incentives, the wow factor can be in the presentation itself: a drum roll, a letter from the president, picture-taking, and plenty of complimentary words. For long-term incentives, the wow needs to be more significant, such as a limo ride to dinner at the nicest restaurant in town or flowers for the award winner's spouse.

Make the awards proportionate to the time frame. You can conduct an incentive program for a day, a quarter, or a year, but the longer the program, the greater the payoff needs to be. People often lose interest in long programs, especially if they are not having winning results.

Shorter programs keep people interested and challenged. The following are examples of awards relative to the length of the incentive program:

One week or less: cash cards in smaller denominations, small gifts, a free lunch, and certificates of achievement.

One to three months: larger cash awards, dinners, social outings (shows, athletic events, cultural attractions), and plaques.

Three months or longer: any of the above items plus trips to popular vacation spots, electronics (such as iPods), and good seats to athletic events or plays.

Focus on results. Keep your incentives simple and straightforward. Don't get complicated. Explain up-front how you will track progress and what the payoff will be. Don't make exceptions or use a complex spreadsheet to compute the numbers. Limit the metrics to three or fewer; any more and the behavioral impact diminishes. If you have too many variables to measure, the results are clouded. Focus on outcomes that help your business or department succeed. Keep your metrics focused on results such as sales, quality, profitability, accounts receivables, customer contacts, add-on sales, follow-ups, higher service ratings, customer retention, and quality.

Communicate, communicate, communicate. Remember: Communication is the foundation of all relationships, and it is critical to the success of incentive programs. Communicate thoroughly at the beginning, in the middle, and at the end of an incentive program. Here are a few examples:

Begin with a kickoff meeting and e-mail follow-up to describe the program: goals, time line, payoff, and tracking.

Create a theme that will create energy and excitement for your team.

Hang posters and distribute flyers.

Give daily, weekly, and monthly updates on results. Make sure everyone is informed.

Do updates in meetings. Share results and success stories, and praise progress.

Get others involved to help support the event, including spouses, customers, the community at large, and other departments. Send out letters and flyers. If appropriate, include them in the recognition.

Use phone conferences to communicate with others separated by distance.

Use pens, hats, shirts, cups, key chains, and banners to help promote the program.

If results are flat or slow coming, conduct refocus meetings that include recognition, problem-solving, opportunities to share ideas, dealing with challenges, retraining, and motivation.

Finally, be an enthusiastic leader. Incentives give you a chance to amplify all of your Superstar leadership skills as you head toward your goals. Be the role model, and do what you are asking others to do. Be the catalyst, cheerleader, and coach for better performance. Help celebrate success. Be an encourager. Overcome barriers to success. Make sure to follow up and follow through. Be highly visible. Most of all, keep your commitments.

Day 22 Superstar Leader Application
Use this worksheet to plan an incentive program for your department.
Goals:
Time Frame:
Theme:
Progress Awards:
Achievement Awards:
Action Steps: 　Team input (time and place): 　Kickoff meeting (time and place): 　Daily tracking (method): 　Training, (on what, by whom, and where): 　Coaching ideas: 　Communication strategies: 　Other:

Leadership and learning are indispensable to each other.

—John F. Kennedy

Day 23
FUN IN THE WORKPLACE

The number-one reason people go to work is because they have to! Their alarm goes off every morning, and they trudge to work. Too many people put in eight, 10, 12 hours a day, year after year, and find no enjoyment in their work. As one manager said, "It's not any fun working here." Why can't it be more fun?

Sam was the VP of training for a large U.S. retailer. For eight years, he traveled from his home on one end of the country to the corporate headquarters on the other end. He did a great job creating a high-performance and enjoyable corporate culture. He developed training programs, incentives, improvement initiatives, and employee-recognition programs for customer service and internal teamwork. He earned the nickname "Doctor of Fun." He always had a smile, hearty laugh, a kind word for others, and a sense of humor. We worked with Sam for a few years. Our philosophies were similar, and together we made a significant improvement in a program for his company's customer service initiatives and bottom line.

Unfortunately, many of the other executives in the company didn't get it. They cared more about Wall Street's analysis, store sales, and profits—and that's what they focused on. The worse the numbers were, the more they pushed and yelled and added metrics and actions step, none of which worked. They didn't understand the High-Performance Formula or the dynamics of a customer loyalty process, nor did they know the elegance of consistently creating a climate that was ripe with recognition, training, coaching, excitement, recognition—and fun!

After a period of time, Sam was asked to retire because he didn't fit their corporate mantra any more. (Just a side note: Many of the other executives left or were fired. The company's stock is dismal, store results are anemic, and they are near bankruptcy.)

How do you create fun in the workplace? With an open mind. Although a company needs to make money, most companies could afford to lighten up a bit. (Thank goodness for "casual day.")

Everything we have discussed thus far will contribute to a more enjoyable work environment. Realistic expectations, fair treatment, learning opportunities, recognition, good coaching, and effective communication will help employees like their jobs more and perform better.

The following three strategies can lighten up the workplace, put some electricity in the air, and create a work atmosphere that is fun, productive, and rewarding:

1. Team activities.
2. Communication activities.
3. Social activities.

Team Activities

All companies have projects that need completion and business segments that need improvement. Teams can be an effective means to get things accomplished. Teams bring out the best in employees— more ideas, stronger commitment, greater involvement, and much more fun. If you get everyone on a team, together they can work on a wide range of business activities, such as:

▸ Accounts receivable.
▸ Sales results.
▸ Service results.
▸ Hiring procedures.
▸ Response time for handling complaints.
▸ Product delivery.
▸ Product quality.
▸ Call center effectiveness.
▸ Training needs.
▸ New product launches.
▸ And other projects: [*list here*].

The list is endless, and the possibilities are great, but beware, lest team processes become boring, burdensome, or overloaded with an endless litany of metrics and procedural review. These very things have bogged down some high-quality business management initiatives. Remember to lighten up a bit, have some fun, and engage your team to capture their hearts and minds.

▸ Name your teams.
▸ Create a banner or logo for every team.

▸ Get polos, t-shirts, and caps embroidered with team names.

▸ Design a colorful goal board for tracking results.

▸ Train employees on how to be an effective team member or leader and on the tasks, processes, and measurement tools of effective teams.

▸ Award team participation or milestones with fantastic prizes.

▸ Track results and give awards for progress and achievement.

Calvin is the service manager for a company in Victoria, British Columbia, with whom we have worked. He has attended a number of the company-sponsored management sessions we have done with his company. He divided his customer service reps into two teams: the Guns and the Roses. They made polos and caps for each team. Throughout the year, they tracked the service and sales results of the teams. In their weekly meetings, they recognized team results and gave team awards. They did team competitions, team cheers, and team training. By year's end, they set company and branch records for results. The two teams were only $1.00 apart in their numbers for the entire year. The reps had a lot of fun, worked hard, achieved excellent results, made extra money, and built lasting camaraderie.

Communication Activities

We have discussed the importance of communication as it relates to one-on-one interactions, but communication needs to go big in order to keep the fun alive. Good communication aimed at increasing the fun factor is like having an internal marketing plan. Just as you attract customers with effective marketing, you need to have a plan for getting your employees' attention. You can promote your team efforts in ways similar to employee recognition, such as the following:

▸ Decorate your work area or lunchroom.

▸ Use bulletin boards to post positive messages.

▸ Hang banners, balloons, and other props that relate to your goals and plans.

▸ Have a wall of fame with employees' pictures and their accomplishments and successes.

▸ Send weekly e-mail messages with some color or pizzazz to encourage and inspire employees to work toward the goals.

▸ Set up a bulletin board or computer dashboard to track results.

▸ Send letters home to spouses or significant others that describe goals.

▶ Use an internal newsletter for recognition, info on plans, updates on progress, and humor.

▶ Hold regular team meetings to discuss progress.

Social Activities

Everyone loves a party, and although we don't suggest partying all the time, there are companies that never loosen up! Americans work more hours than employees in any other country around the world. Yet 75 percent of all American workers say they would quit their jobs if they could. The truth is that uptight employees don't do the best work.

Recently, a flight attendant for a major U.S. airline said, "I hate people. They are just like cattle. All I want to do is serve them quickly and get away from them and read my book."

Whoa! Maybe that was just one worker's opinion. We would hope so, too, however, while we were at a hotel near the world headquarters of this (unnamed) airline, we noticed the same airline's graduation exercises for a new class of flight attendants in an adjoining meeting room. During a break, we went over and told one of their leaders, "This is nice to see."

His matter-of-fact reply was, "No, you don't understand; this is 40 more votes for the union." That airline has serious morale and service issues. It, like many airlines, went through bankruptcy.

Can't people have fun and do a great job, too? Professional athletes play their childhood games for a livelihood; they excel and seem to hold on to the fun. Because we spend a good portion of our lives on the job, we need to make it more enjoyable while achieving the corporate objectives.

There are many possible social activities. Choose the ones that work for the people you employ.

- Holiday parties (the most common).
- Lunch meetings.
- Comedy club dinners.
- Ball games.
- Zoo days.
- Goof-off days.
- Museum days.
- Surprise parties.
- Nice dinners.
- Retreats.
- Training meetings in warm-weather locations.
- After-work pizza.
- Practical jokes in the office (within reason).
- Skits to present ideas.
- On-site recognition days.

You end up with mediocre performance if you and your employees do the same old, same old every day. You can't do all of these things all of the time, but with some common sense and propriety, you can intermix these kinds of activities in the work environment to help everyone feel more valued and appreciated. You can tap into tremendous employee potential using the strategies we've discussed. Remember what motivates people and what gives them a sense of purpose. Show them respect, and express your appreciation for jobs well done. Make use of every opportunity to make both work and learning fun. The payoff will be worth it.

Day 23 Superstar Leader Application
Describe how you can achieve greater performance while having more fun at work through the following strategies.
Team activities.
Communication activities.
Social activities.

Effective leadership is putting first things first. Effective management is discipline, carrying it out.

—Stephen Covey

FOCUSING ON CONTINUOUS IMPROVEMENT IN QUALITY AND SERVICE

Day 24
PROACTIVE
PLANNING

Customer service seems to be on the decline in all industries. It's been said, "Service stinks everywhere," and it almost seems useless to complain about lousy service. Yet research shows improved customer service that outshines the competition will help a business be more profitable. Organizations such as the following have proven that better customer service pays off:

▶ U.S. Office of Consumer Affairs.

▶ Strategic Planning Institute.

▶ Malcolm Baldrige Award.

▶ JD Power.

▶ American Customer Satisfaction Index, Michigan Ross School of Business.

Continuous improvement in operations is a high priority for Superstar leaders; improvement comes with better quality, better service, and pride in a job well done. Bad bosses either don't give this concept much thought or they simply fail to act.

Improvement is not optional to remain viable in business today. Most businesses work with moving targets—stronger competitors, new products, improved technologies, and change in general. Managers need to find ways to do things better, faster, or differently. For years, retail giant Sears was the industry leader, but the company got comfortable and failed to maintain an ongoing improvement mentality. Consequently, Sears went through some tough times until it chose to reinvent itself. The improvements brought the company back to life—maybe not as the leader but definitely as a strong player.

In our consulting, we have discovered most managers are pitifully unprepared to improve service or quality. Business seems to go on as usual for most company leaders, especially at the middle management level. Very few leaders look at the bigger picture.

The most successful businesses, such as Intel, Disney, Southwest Airlines, and Walgreens, have developed a corporate culture of innovation that focuses on improvement. Unfortunately, many American businesses lack what Japanese businesses call "kaizen," an attitude and process of continuous improvement.

According to Dr. Leonard Barry at the Texas A&M University, customers have specific wants and expectations that can be summarized by these five factors:

1. **Responsiveness**—prompt and efficient service.

2. **Assurance**—knowledgeable and capable service people who are able to get the job done.

3. **Tangibles**—well-groomed employees, a professional and attractive business environment, and the proper tools for providing service.

4. **Reliability**—consistency and follow-through.

5. **Empathy**—care, concern, and willingness to go the extra mile for the customer.[1]

In the end, customers want great service, great quality, and great prices; they want it all. Neither companies nor managers can afford to ignore this fact. Many talk about service or quality, but few really do it well. It's easy to wonder why managers don't focus on the factors that can make a huge difference in both customer and employee satisfaction.

Research done by quality-service icons Deming, Crosby, and Juran have led the way to show that improved quality and service will save and make you money.

We believe that 85–95 percent of quality or service problems are management-related. Employees are not doing well because management has failed to provide the tools, training, support, equipment, recognition, teamwork, and so forth to help them excel. Management often gets in the way of people who want to do a good job.

Superstar leaders get into action. Superstar leaders find ways to improve and in time make it a habit. Bad bosses don't naturally see that anything needs to be done, so they simply tend to do more of the same, harder.

In our work with numerous North American and worldwide businesses, we have seen that customer service or quality improvements begin with good planning. The most important aspects of effective and ongoing improvement are the thought process, communication, and problem-solving. It is the critical and creative look at what a business is doing and determining how to do it better. It's listening to both customers and employees—and then getting to work. One tool to help in the planning process is the SWOT analysis.

SWOT Analysis

What Is It?

SWOT analysis is used to identify and analyze the Strengths and Weaknesses of your organization, as well as the Opportunities and Threats revealed by the information you gather from your external or internal environments. You can gather the data from customer feedback surveys, quality reports, financial reports, customer or client communication, observations, and employees.

Who Uses It?

Managers, management teams, and team leaders or members of continuous improvement teams.

Why Use It?

To develop a continuous improvement plan that utilizes the best information you have from internal and external sources about your company's or department's strengths, opportunities, weaknesses, and threats. The goal is to enhance the strengths and opportunities while protecting you from weaknesses or threats. One company we worked with implemented a continuous improvement plan and doubled its business in a less than a decade.

When to Use It?

To help you improve because of problems you are facing or in an effort to proactively get better in response to a vision or goals. The structure will help you review and analyze your external environment (for example, the culture, economy, competition, complaints, and customer feedback) or your internal environment (for example, training, budget, teamwork, culture, and procedures).

Hot to Use It?

1. **Internal Review:** Examine the capabilities of your organization or department. This can be done by analyzing your organization's strengths and weaknesses.

2. **External Review:** Look at outside forces such as customers, competitors, the economy, and so on in your analysis, and identify areas of potential opportunities for your team and those that signify threats or obstacles to success.

3. Use the Proactive Planning form and the various parts that relate to your job.

4. Use the review to create goals and action steps to minimize weaknesses and threats, and maximize strengths and opportunities.

5. Gain input and involvement from others to help expand your information and creativity.

Day 24 Superstar Leader Application
Use this outline as a starting point for a continuous improvement plan in your areas of responsibility. Include your employees in the planning process, and update your plans quarterly. The categories in this guide are only examples; list your own as needed. Analyze data and information that relate to your effectiveness, and then establish goals and action steps for improvement.

Key Considerations for Customer Needs
Problems/complaints. Customer feedback data. Relationship to customers. Knowledge of products. Marketing support or research. Business priorities for customer segments. Other: [list here].

S.W.O.T. Analysis for Customer Needs
What are our strengths?
What are our weaknesses?

What are the opportunities?
What are the threats?

Key Goals/Plans for Customer Needs

Priority strengths (identify three to five).
Priority weaknesses to improve (identify two to three).
Priority opportunities (identify one to two).
Priority threats to neutralize (identify one to two).

Key Considerations for Employee Needs

Labor issues.
Training opportunities.
Coaching challenges.
Teamwork.
Benefits and compensation.
Recruiting and hiring practices.
Other: [*list here*].

S.W.O.T. Analysis for Employee Needs

What are our strengths?

What are our weaknesses?

What are the opportunities?

What are the threats?

Key Goals/Plans for Employee Needs
Priority strengths (identify three to five).
Priority weaknesses to improve (identify two to three).
Priority opportunities (identify one to two).
Priority threats to neutralize (identify one to two).
S.M.A.R.T.goals (list three to five).
Action Steps: (list here)

Before you are a leader, success is all about growing yourself. When you become a leader, success is all about growing others.

—Jack Welch

Day 25
PROBLEM-SOLVING

Managers face serious challenges today. Which ones do you face?

- Grow the business.
- Raise sales.
- Increase customer service.
- Decrease turnover.
- Engage employees.
- Improve morale.
- Deal with a diverse workforce.
- Reduce costs.
- Keep customers.
- Defeat competition around the world and at home.
- Manage performance results.
- Create a learning organization.
- Enhance productivity.
- Communicate from a distance.
- Drive innovation.

Of course, in today's market, once this is accomplished, managers must then focus on continuous improvement, and do it all again with a smaller budget—sometimes.

Tom is the owner of business in Indianapolis. He has six locations and does about $400 million a year. He says the number-one thing he looks for in leaders is whether or not they take initiative. He further explained that he needs managers who can look at their situation, analyze it, create a plan, make a decision, and take action with a sense of urgency.

Managers need to be proactive problem-solvers. However, two comments we often hear about managers today are:

▶ They lack follow-through. They talk about what they will do but never do it.

▶ You can never find a manager when you need one. Then nothing ever changes and the problems get bigger.

Too many managers are seen as aloof and uninvolved in their businesses, or are seen as micromanagers. Both are extremes. A manager is effective if his or her people are effective. If everyone on the team is focused on proactive problem-solving, everyone wins.

Here are two steps to remember:

First, minimize problems and solve problems before they become dire by taking initiative. Don't wait for your boss to ask you to create a plan. (Use our outline for planning as a guide.) Size up your department or business; get input from your team. Always stay a step ahead of the game. If your boss does yearly planning, do quarterly planning. If your boss does quarterly planning, do monthly planning. If your boss wants reports with results on Tuesday, be prepared by Monday. Why? It's proactive and shows initiative. Always temper this with the needs of your customers, employees, and the business in mind. The important thing here is you have an attitude that focuses on thinking through what you need to do to win in your job, making a decision, and then acting on it. That's what a good boss does. Bad bosses shoot from the hip or wait for others to tell them what to do.

Second, follow the problem-solving process:

Identify the problem. What is it really? What shows up may be a symptom. For example, if your customer service results are low, it could mean your employees aren't well trained. It could also mean you haven't clarified expectations. It could mean you haven't followed up on your expectations.

Get the facts. Make some notes on the details of the problem. For example, with the issue of low customer service results, review your customer complaint data. Also, talk to customers yourself and get direct input. Observe your employees in action with customers. Hold a meeting with employees and review their understanding of your standards and expectations. In other words, do your homework.

Create possible alternative solutions. Brainstorm possible action steps to solve the problem. It's a good idea to get input from others to help you. Hold a brainstorm session with your team. Ask other managers for ideas. Pick your solutions based on priority, and set a goal for results and improvement.

Make an action plan. Next, make some decisions. Establish a measureable goal. List five to seven action steps for improvement. Add some time lines, and review dates so you can check on progress. Then do it.

In some cases, you will document this process like you do with your overall plan for improvement. In other cases, it's a thinking process that you do quickly, decide, and then act on. For example, if you need to improve your order-processing system for customer orders, you will need a more detailed planning process. This is a more complex process, and it will take time to think it through, assess the needs, and put a plan in place for improvement. On the other hand, if you have a customer complaint, you have a greater sense of urgency to make a decision and get it handled. You might solve the problem on the spot, but use the outline to guide your thinking. Or you may need to investigate the issue and get back to the customer later in the day or the next day. Again, the process can guide you.

Coaching Employees to be Problem-Solvers

William Oncken wrote the book *Managing Management Time: Who's Got the Monkey?*[1] Too many times, employees have problems—monkeys—and they seek out the boss to solve it. The employee reviews the problem with the boss and leaves it with the boss to solve. Before you know it, the manager has all of the problems—monkeys—and not enough time to solve them.

Here's how it plays out:

Sam, a supervisor, comes to you because he has an employee with a performance problem. He tells you the employee isn't doing his job. Many managers respond by saying, *"I will talk to the employee."* Sam walks away, and who now has the problem? When Sam has another problem, what will he do? He will give it to his manager—you.

Instead, try this approach:

Sam, a supervisor, comes to you with the employee problem. Ask a series of questions:

"Sam, describe the performance issue in terms of results."

"How often is it happening?"

"What have you said to, and done with, the employee so far?"

"How has the employee responded?"

"What do you think you should do next? How do you think the employee will respond?"

"Is there any other alternative?" (Add any suggestions at this point.)

"What action will you take and why?"

"Let me know how it works out."

Now if Sam has poor thinking or alternatives, you can give guidance and direction, or get a human resources representative involved with a discipline or firing situation to make sure you do it right. But, notice who has the responsibility for the problem: Sam. Who are you teaching how to solve problems? Sam. By doing this consistently when your employees come to you with problems, you only need to ask a couple of questions:

> ▶ What are the details of the situation?

> ▶ What are you thinking needs to be done?

Eventually, they will just solve the problems, and when you have a one-on-one session, they will inform you of the results. It's been said, "The only ones without problems are six feet under." Problems are the name of the game. Managers need to be problem-solvers. They need to be proactive problem-solvers and decision-makers. If you take the approach as described, your performance will be noticed by upper management because, instead of stewing or worrying about problems, you and your people are solving them.

Day 25 Superstar Leader Application
Identify a problem you are faced with and describe it:
What are the facts?
What are the possible solutions?
What action will you take?
How will you measure success?

Difficulties are opportunities to better things; they are stepping-stones to greater experience.... When one door closes, another always opens; as a natural law it has to balance.

—Brian Adams

Day 26
INNOVATION IN THE WORKPLACE

Today, many of our organizations are in a survival mode. Cost-cutting, conserving cash, and protecting shareholder value are the focus. Some high-velocity organizations have learned how to maintain their lead ahead of the competition, but many companies are losing their energy and vitality.

It is our belief that innovation is one of the keys to a thriving, growing organization. Innovation is about doing our work in new and better ways—fostering a thinking process that delivers improvements not possible before. To take this one step further, it is our belief that, as managers and leaders, we need to take the concept of innovation and make it our behavior. Mergers, cost-cutting, downsizing, benchmarking, reorganization, and reengineering work, but you eventually reach a point of diminishing returns because when you look up and turn around, you discover that all of your competitors are doing the same things.

We as leaders can learn how to encourage change and create engagement in the most complex of organizations. We can learn how to bring out the best thinking of our greatest asset: our people. We can learn how to encourage a climate that engages the whole organization in growth.

This section is about new thinking and new solutions to move our organizations forward. It is about us becoming leaders who nurture and encourage innovation. It is about us discovering the changes we need to make personally to foster innovation all around us. This day's subject is about how we think, about better thinking, and about being open to new ideas so that we can leave a legacy of growth in our departments or organizations. The implication is that we can incorporate innovative leadership into all levels of our company.

The bottom line is that innovation creates wealth. We all know that innovation in Silicon Valley has created billions of dollars in new wealth. But innovation also creates benefits for you as a leader. If you are seen as a leader who encourages and nurtures innovation, you will have more influence with those around you, you will become a model for leadership, more opportunities will open up for you, and you will accomplish more.

The number-one issue facing organizations today is clarity.

▶ Where are we going?

▶ What's my role?

▶ How do I fit in?

▶ What's my future?

Innovation offers leaders the opportunity, at all levels, to provide that clarity to their organization. We can invite all employees to participate in the delivery of an organizational promise built around innovation. Innovation creates a rich purpose for an organization that drives change and creates engagement in even the most complex of organizations. It invites the best thinking from people. It encourages and creates a climate that involves the whole organization in growth. A vision that inspires every employee to make your organization more innovative will inspire every employee if it is genuine and authentic.

The questions then become: How do we make new thinking and innovation happen in our company? How do we replicate it? How do we make it part of our processes? What are the elements of leadership that make innovation happen? How do we encourage our employees to bring their best thinking to work every day?

We believe that the best place to start is to appreciate the innovation that is already occurring. It is important to understand and celebrate the creative victories that you have already had, in order to understand what the process is and what can be replicated. Organizations always move ahead faster if we build on the successes that they have already had.

Once we have helped the organization discover that innovation is already occurring, we can then begin to focus on the behaviors we want to encourage in the organization. As leaders, we need to start with our own behaviors and model them for the organization.

The following graphic on page 175 provides a short summary of the behaviors we need to internalize, demonstrate, and live to encourage a climate of innovation, starting in our own areas of responsibility. These behaviors provide a clear and relatively simple model for any leader to follow who wants to create a dynamic, growing, innovative, learning organization.

Superstar leaders start with the premise that the climate for our organizations begins with us; we can then focus on the behaviors we need to model for the organization. It's about us, as leaders, taking responsibility for our behaviors, creating accountability for our behaviors, taking on the responsibility that our behaviors need to change, measuring those behaviors and results, and recognizing that innovation and our leadership behaviors are the future of this organization. In contrast, too many bosses stay content with the status quo doing the same old thing every day.

Leadership Behaviors to Grow
Through a Climate of Innovation

Listens
- *Asks relevant questions.*
- *Employees/customers.*

Provides Clarity
- *Simplifies, makes expectations clear.*
- *Articulates where organization is going.*

#1 issue is growth

Making our company the most innovative enterprise is the key to growth

To grow we need to take the concept of innovation and express it throught our behaviors

Coaches
- *Formally.*
- *In the moment.*
- *Thinks of self as model.*

Recognizes and Rewards
- *Uses every opportunity.*

In the end, it's about how you choose to behave that determines if the organization wins. With this realization, we learn that leadership means personal engagement, encouraging the best of our collective thinking, listening to our organization and our customers, and creating a focus and clarity for our organization.

What Can You Do, as a Boss, to Encourage Innovation?

The premise of this chapter is that it is your behavior as a leader that sets the tone for innovation in your work group. WCW has actually proven this premise in 3M, often recognized as one of the world's most innovative companies. We have identified 10 leadership behaviors that are actually proven to increase innovation in a work group.

These leadership behaviors are:

1. **Make a commitment to personal discovery.** Am I modeling the behavior of personal growth and discovery?
2. **Make a commitment to being vulnerable.** Am I taking risks, innovating, and being vulnerable to those around me in this process?
3. **Make a commitment to being open.** Am I being open to what's around me and in the process allowing new opportunities to be available to me?

4. **Make a commitment to dialogue.** Am I taking to time to talk with people and allowing the good thinking of others to be available to me?
5. **Make a commitment to the highest intent of the group.** Do I trust that my work group wants only the best for themselves and is bringing that to the workplace every day?
6. **Make a commitment to contribution.** Am I allowing everyone's contribution to be made?
7. **Make a commitment to inclusion.** Am I including everyone in the work and thinking of the group?
8. **Make a commitment to caring.** Does everyone in the workgroup feel that I care about them?
9. **Make a commitment to helping.** Am I helping everyone in the workgroup make a successful contribution?
10. **Make a commitment to belief.** Do I believe in the abilities of everyone in the workgroup?

Superstar leaders strive to create a work environment that allows people to express themselves. They seek to tap their greatest ideas. The questions give you ways of doing this. Poor leaders give no thought to this at all.

(**Note:** We thank Bruce Moorhouse, our business partner, for his contribution on this. He spent 29 years working with 3M on innovation.)

Day 26 Superstar Leader Application
Have you had a discussion with your team about what innovation means to the group?
Have you identified and celebrated the innovations that have already happened?
Have you asked the group about what they believe the innovative behaviors are?
Have you created a vision for your group around innovation?

To be creative you have to contribute something different from what you've done before. Your results need not be original to the world; few results truly meet that criterion. In fact, most results are built on the work of others.

—Lynne C. Levesque

HIRING
THE BEST PEOPLE

DAY 27: Recruiting and Hiring Winners

Day 27
RECRUITING AND HIRING WINNERS

Your success as a manager is often linked to how well you recruit and hire. Unfortunately, not all managers have complete control over the selection process, and some managers inherit the employees they oversee. At times, corporate or human resources policies make it difficult to hire the best candidates, or the best talent isn't interested in the job. In both good and bad hiring situations, the Superstar leadership strategies are critical.

The selection process is a crucial element of a high-performance strategy. Managers need to understand good selection practices because the best managers tend to have the best people. A successful working relationship is a combination of good selection practices and strong employee development. Unfortunately, many managers use poor, outdated, inadvertently illegal, and sometimes harmful recruitment methods that put their companies at great risk.

Turnover is a pain, and if you are constantly training new employees, you regularly lose ground. As we have stated, the wrong hire can cost three times the annual salary. Those kinds of turnover costs can negatively impact the department or company. High turnover rates suggest that management, through poor hiring habits, is missing opportunities for better service, sales, quality, or profit.

Following are some of the most unusual things that happened during job interviews. As you read the list, consider your response to these potential new hires.

▶ The candidate wore a business suit with flip-flops.
▶ The candidate asked if the interviewer wanted to meet for a drink afterward.
▶ The candidate had applied for an accounting job, yet said he or she was "bad at managing money."
▶ The candidate ate food in the employee break room after the interview.
▶ The candidate recited poetry.

- The candidate applying for a customer service job said, "I don't really like working with people."
- The candidate had to go immediately to get his or her dog that had gotten loose in the parking lot.
- The candidate looked at the ceiling during the entire interview.
- The candidate used Dungeons & Dragons as an example of teamwork.
- The candidate clipped his or her fingernails.[1]

Hiring good people begins with a commitment to always be recruiting. If you only recruit when you need someone, it takes longer to fill empty positions, and you may take shortcuts or make mistakes in your effort to get the job filled. The highly competitive job market is not going anywhere; there are not enough talented people to go around. As Baby Boomers retire, recruiting and hiring winners is even more crucial. Today's generation of workers understands this and is making more demands. Companies are becoming more creative in their recruiting strategies with options such as the following:

- Use of social media (LinkedIn, blogging, and so forth).
- Recruiting bonuses.
- Signing bonuses.
- Flexible benefits.
- Home offices.
- Internships.
- Educational programs.
- Emphasizing work/life balance.
- Hosting group events such as water rafting, skiing, or ropes courses.

Managers engaged in ongoing recruiting can benefit from the following well-tested recruitment methods:

- **Networking.** Talk to talented people through your normal networking channels. Keep a file, and ask for recommendations.
- **Internal candidates.** Keep in contact with people within your company; they can be good prospects.
- **Associations.** Join professional associations in your areas of expertise to find new leads.

▶ **College campuses.** Get on campus to find new talent.

▶ **Internet.** Search on-line through the many different job-posting services or social media sites.

▶ **Want ads.** Tried and true, the newspaper is still a respectable source.

▶ **Job agencies.** Recruiting is their expertise, and they charge about one-third of the new hire's salary (employee or employer paid).

▶ **Public job service programs.** Free programs that tend to generate lesser quality leads.

You will find most of the job candidates you need through networking or from within your own company. However, social media methods are rapidly growing in effectiveness and popularity.

A methodical and practical selection process is important. We recommend four simple steps:

1. Prepare to hire right.
2. Create a positive communication climate.
3. Conduct a professional interview.
4. Evaluate all candidates objectively.

Prepare to Hire Right

We say preparation and determination are all-powerful. Preparation is especially true for hiring. It starts with two written documents: an updated job description and a set of preliminary job goals. A job description provides an overview of the position and lists job duties. A list of preliminary job goals should include three to five SMART goals that will measure success in their first three months on the job.

It is important to review the job description and job goals with every candidate. Human resources law is very particular; the interview is the "test" that any new hire must pass and the interviewer deliver consistently and fairly. These two documents set the standard by which candidates can be judged. They help remove bias in the interview process.

Additionally, as reviewed, the majority of job performance problems stem from a lack of clear expectations and goals. Those problems can be minimized if candidates know the expectations of the job for which they are being considered.

Early in the hiring process, it is necessary to determine the kind of person you want in the job. What qualities are you looking for? Evaluate people already in similar positions, or use assessment tools to identify preferred traits. (Several reputable companies sell personality assessment tools that can be useful.) At the very least, make a list of the primary qualities, educational background, skills, and work experience you require for the position. Use this list to help you formulate questions for the interview and during the decision-making process.

Create a Positive Communication Climate

Remember that the best candidates are investigating you and your company during an interview as much as you are checking them out. Good communication techniques will help you sell yourself as a manager. Review Day 8 as you prepare for interviews, and consider these points specific to the interview process:

▶ **Be prepared.** Have your materials ready, including the job description and goals, and relevant company literature. Make sure to review it all before the interview and not during it.

▶ **Be on time.** This shows you value the person's time.

▶ **Find privacy for the interview.** Avoid cubicles, noisy factory settings, crowded restaurants, and other noisy or public settings.

▶ **Greet the candidate positively.** Shake hands; offer a chair and something to drink.

▶ **Be courteous and polite.** Simply be respectful.

▶ **Use the person's name once or twice.** People like to hear their own name.

▶ **Make a little small talk.** Talk about the weather, sports, or something in the news for a few minutes.

▶ **Watch your body language.** Sit up straight and make eye contact.

▶ **Sit to the side of the candidate.** Position the candidate's chair so it is not directly in front of you, or sit at a table. This is less intimidating and more personable.

▶ **Be a good listener.** You will learn much by how people answer questions as well as by what they don't say.

Your goal should be to help candidates feel comfortable and relaxed. If they are relaxed, they will be more honest and straightforward in their discussion with you. These simple steps also give you and your company credibility.

Conduct a Professional Interview

You can do an interview in one of three ways: by intimidation, haphazardly, or professionally. The intimidation method usually involves the boss and a large posse of people grilling the candidate for hours with innumerable questions. The haphazard method occurs when the manager is unprepared, late, or otherwise unsure of the plan. Both are unprofessional. Bad bosses tend to use these methods without a thought. Superstar leaders use a professional, business-like approach that begins with words such as the following:

"Let me give you an overview of how this interview will proceed. I am going to ask you some questions. I will then explain the job in detail. Then you can ask me your questions, and I might have a few more. It should take us from 45 minutes to an hour. After that, I will have you talk to my colleague. Then we will touch base for a few more minutes and talk about the next steps. How does that sound to you? Great, let's begin. My first question is...."

It is important to mention the next steps so candidates know what will happen. Tell them if you are interviewing more people. Let them know the time frame for your final decision. Let them know if there is the possibility for a second round of interviews. Provide as much information as possible without revealing your decision on the spot (even if you are sure you will/ will not hire the person). Many managers conduct phone interviews to save time. In phone interviews, your goal is to check the following:

1. Use the phone interview to screen applicants. This will save you time.

2. Be prepared.

3. Make a list of questions. Focus on the requirements of the job (education, technical skills, years of experience, and so forth).

4. Schedule the call, and call on time. You should be able to do the interview in 15–30 minutes.

5. Review your hiring process and expectations of the applicant.

The major disadvantage to phone interviews is your inability to observe how the candidates nonverbally react to your questions. The major advantage is it saves you time.

If possible, apply the "rule of three" to all your interviewing efforts: Interview candidates three times—with three different people in three different settings. This takes more time, but it will give you better information for your hiring decision. Including other people also helps you avoid common hiring hazards such as:

▸ **Biases and prejudices.** We all have them.

▸ **Halo/horn effect.** One good or bad fact about the person or the person's experience cements our overall impression.

▸ **Missing information.** No one can remember everything. Take notes on a piece of paper that can be thrown away after the decision is made. Don't write on the resume or application, as that will need to remain on file.

▸ **Misinterpreting information.** Getting others involved can help you double check (or eliminate) your assumptions and make a better decision.

▸ **Hiring too quickly.** You have a spot to fill and you need someone, so the first person who looks good and can breathe, you want to hire.

Always make a question list before the interview to ensure that you are consistent with what you ask from one candidate to the next. Your questions should relate to the education and experience or background required for the job, the job duties, and your performance expectations. Ask each candidate to complete an application, and review it before the interview. The application can answer basic questions you won't need to ask. (The resume is the candidate's sales tool.)

You can add informational questions to help you assess education and experience such as the following:

"Tell me about your college experience."

"Tell me about yourself."

"Tell me about your last job or current job."

"Why do you want to leave your current job?"

"What are your strengths?"

"Where can you improve?"

"What motivates you?"

"Why are you interested in our company?"

"What do you want in a new job?"

"What kind of supervision do you need?"

"Why should we hire you?"

Behavior questions focus on technical and relationship aspects of the job. The following examples can be made more specific to the job for which you are hiring. Your goal is for candidates to describe real situations they have encountered in past jobs that relate to the position you need to fill.

"Describe the details of a presentation you made in the past."

"Tell me how you handle demanding and difficult customers."

"Give me an example of an application problem you had in your department and how you resolved it."

"Describe the decision-making authority you have had in the recent past."

"Give me an example of a tough decision you had to make and the results."

"Tell me how you have handled chronically late employees."

"Describe a time you had to fire someone. How did you do it?"

"Give me an example of a departmental goal that you didn't achieve. What happened, and how did you handle it?"

"Describe a time you helped speed up the product development cycle."

"Give me an example of a project you led and how you managed the process."

Avoid the following in your questions; it's the law.

▶ Marital status and/or number of children.

▶ Race, religion, natural country, native language.

▶ Height, weight, hair and eye color, pregnancy.

▶ Age. (You may only ask if the candidate is over the age of 18; if hiring teens, you need to know how various child labor laws apply.)

▶ U.S. citizenship.

▶ Disabilities. (Employers are required to make reasonable accommodations for all candidates.)

▶ Education level. (Education level can be discussed if you can demonstrate that success on the job requires a certain level of education.)

▶ Questions relating to arrests or any type of military discharge.

186 | SUPERSTAR LEADERSHIP

Evaluate Objectively

You have five main resources to guide your hiring decisions: applications and/or resumes, interviews, reference checks, other interviewers, and assessment tools.

Application/resume. Do the candidates' experience, skills, and education fit the job? Is the application complete and neat? Are there any gaps in employment that need to be explained?

Interviews. How well do the candidates answer the questions? How do the candidates handle themselves during the interview? How did their appearance fit the job? Are there any red flags? What do the other interviewers think?

Reference checks. Do the reference checks verify employment? Do the checks reveal any red flags? Check three references to verify employment because people can lie. Unfortunately, it isn't possible to know what's true and what isn't simply from the application or resume.

The following is a step-by-step guide for checking references.

1. Call the candidate's company. Avoid human resources (HR) or personnel departments; call the candidate's supervising manager. Call HR to confirm employee if that is your only option.

2. Identify yourself and why you are calling. Ask to verify the employment of [*candidate's name*].

3. Ask about the candidate's strengths and what could have been done better.

4. Ask, manager to manager, how the candidate was supervised.

5. Ask the manager if the candidate would be hired again.

Call professional contacts, too; they will be most informative. Be very polite. Say thank you. Sometimes you have to read between the lines of what is said. Everyone worries about lawsuits, and company policies often restrict the information that can be released, but if you follow less-formal channels, as described, you will likely get more information. Listen carefully, and you will hear what you need to know to make good hiring decisions.

Assessment tools. More companies today are using assessment tools, but they should not be used as the sole criteria for hiring. They provide additional information. There are many assessments available online. If you choose to use them, apply the information fairly and consistently with all candidates.

In the end, hiring decisions must be based on a combination of all these elements. Gather input from everyone who participated in the process. (A rating form or matrix might be helpful for making comparisons.) Finally, consider these qualities in candidates:

▸ **Job match.** Does the candidate fit the minimum skills, education, and experience for the job?

▸ **Past performance.** Does the candidate's history of work and education relate to the job?

▸ **Achievement.** Does the candidate show evidence of success, progress, and accomplishment?

▸ **Work ethic.** Does the candidate seem to be willing and able to work hard?

▸ **Good questions.** Does the candidate ask good questions (questions not related to money and benefits)?

▸ **"I want it."** Does the person imply or explicitly say, "I want this job," and seem enthusiastic about the opportunity?

Send a letter of thanks to candidates who are not selected as soon as possible. Here is a sample letter:

Dear Kelli,

Thank you for your interest and application to ABC Company for the position of customer service rep. We have carefully reviewed your experience and background, and although your track record is admirable, we have decided to pursue another direction and cannot offer you employment at this time.

We wish you success in your job search and will keep your resume on file for one year. Thank you again for your interest in our organization.

Sincerely Yours,

188 | SUPERSTAR LEADERSHIP

It is also advisable to send a letter to applicants who submitted resumes but did not receive additional consideration.

Once the hiring decision is made, call the candidates or put together a written offer (in the case of professional positions). Any offer should spell out the details of the job, including job title, start date, compensation, pay procedures, salary review process, initial employment period, overview of benefits, and training that will be provided. Superstar leaders engage in effective hiring practices and recruitment. Bad bosses shoot from the hip in the hiring process—and beyond—and they consequently have higher employee turnover. Superstar leaders have a plan and stick to it. They attract and hire better performers, and then they work to bring out their employees' best. The results they achieve are quite often impressive.

You can be a better boss. The opportunity is yours. Take hold of it.

Day 27 Superstar Leader Application
What are the best strategies you have used for recruiting and hiring?
What did you learn or relearn in this section?

I hire people brighter than me and then I get out of their way.

—Lee Iacocca

PUTTING IT ALL INTO PRACTICE

DAY 28: Superstar Learnings

Day 29: Superstar Action Plans

Day 30: Execution Excellence

Day 31: In Summary: The Superstar Leadership Presence

Day 28
SUPERSTAR
LEARNINGS

Motivator Zig Ziglar once said, "The greatest enemy of excellence is good."

Congratulations! You've stayed the course by reading this book and working the applications. By doing the reading and immediately applying the concepts to your current management practices and committing to trying out new ideas, you've started on the path toward becoming a good boss, maybe even a Superstar leader. During these last three days of material, we will recap what you've learned and help you pull it all together. Plus, we have a bonus with a section on a leader's presence. In addition, we dare you to achieve greater heights.

This section is titled Superstar Learnings to encourage you to capture what you learned from this book. What new concepts or skills did you learn or relearn? What new ideas came to mind? What new behaviors or management practices have you implemented?

Too many employees today still gather after work hours with compatriots to complain about their bosses. A magazine (we haven't been able to locate the source) received more than 6,000 responses to its request for people to submit the reasons they hated their bosses. The list included the following reasons:

- Communicates poorly.
- Tells lies.
- Indecisive.
- Favors "brown nosers."
- Does not listen.
- Procrastinates.
- Forgetful.
- Withholds information.
- Belittles employees.
- Talks too much.

One employee said he hated his boss because he imitated "Mr. Magoo" too often. Another said he hated his boss because his false teeth flopped around when he talked. Yet another claimed he hated his boss because he shot needles at a target on the back of his office door. The reasons range from sensible to ridiculous. Yet there are some weird things going on out there in the name of leadership. Diligently applying the concepts in this book will help you become a good, better, or potentially Superstar leader, but it's up to you. We believe it's the managers who must get results in their areas of responsibility.

> ▶ Managers must bring out the best—not beat or bribe out the best—in their employees to get results. We believe managers are responsible for a work environment that cultivates high performance and that feels good.

> ▶ Managers must find innovative ways to improve performance to achieve better results if not great results.

This takes time, persistence, and commitment. A commitment is a steadfast resolve to do something no matter what. It took commitment to get this far in this book. If you have tried some of the different approaches we've discussed, we are confident you are seeing employees respond positively. Keep at it. Consistency is a key to performance improvement. Your employees will watch to see if your changed behaviors will last. They want to know if you will recognize their hard work again or just one time. Your credibility will be harmed if you start and stop, and lack consistency. Your employees will lose their trust if you don't follow through effectively, and the result will be an unwillingness to do their jobs well. As you apply what you have learned over time, your employees will trust your intentions and respond brilliantly to your efforts.

Marc is a manager for a business in Ottawa. He began applying the Superstar Leadership Strategies immediately after attending a three-day company region meeting. He saw improved results within a few weeks, and he ended up with his best quarter ever. He had a union to contend with, and he was challenged on some of his initiatives to increase goals, communicate with one-on-ones, hold regular training, and so on, but Marc persevered. Over time, his employees' attitudes changed, and in the next year his employees achieved results that were 195 percent beyond their previous performance. Wow!

Marc's behaviors changed as much as the employees' attitudes changed; together, they exceeded their goals. First, he started doing things differently, and then, the employees performed better. You and your employees can do likewise. Do the following Superstar Leader Application thoughtfully and completely.

Day 28 Superstar Leader Application
Describe what have you learned or relearned on each of the following topics:
Motivating people.
Setting clear goals and expectations.
Giving positive feedback and recognition.
Communicating positively and proactively.
Leading with flexibility.
Delivering effective training.
Coaching with excellence.
Creating incentives and fun.
Focusing on continuous improvement in quality and service.
Recruiting and hiring winners.

Great moments are born from great opportunities.

—Herb Brooks

Day 29
SUPERSTAR
ACTION PLANS

It's been said that "Action, not knowledge, is power." If an architect designs a skyscraper, it has little use unless it is built. If you watch a video about improving your golf game, it's useless unless you practice what you've learned on the golf course. As we have described, Daniel Goleman's research suggests that IQ doesn't determine your success in life; it's your emotional intelligence—social and personal competence—in your interactions with others.

Success as a leader is about people, too. All of what we have discussed and worked on is about people. First, it was about you and developing your leadership skills. Second, about your team (or, the team you may have one day) and the affect you have on others. The Superstar Leader Applications throughout this book have encouraged you to take action and to change in positive ways. Practical examples have been given to guide you to consistent execution. Also, research evidence of success has been provided to encourage, to act, and to follow through. Now it's time to create an action plan to cement your new skills and ideas into strong, constructive management habits that will help you discover sensational results! This action plan needs to apply directly to your job, and it needs to employ the KISS principle: Keep It Simple and Straightforward.

It's been said that business strategic plans are often worthless. But strategic planning is crucial. In other words, the actual plan may not be fully useful because things can change rapidly, but the process of critically reviewing what's happening in a business and envisioning what you want to become is priceless. An action plan is more about the thought process behind it than the actual document that is produced.

Your action plan can be formatted according to our example or as you choose, but be thoughtful in your approach to this exercise. Too many managers become reactive to the challenges they face because they have failed to plan. They blame the market, the customers, the employees, and everyone but themselves for their lack of planning. Superstar leaders are as busy as anyone, but they make time for planning.

Taking the initiative to analyze their company, department, or customers; focusing on their priorities; setting goals; and establishing action steps separate the excellent managers from the rest. Analyzing your own leadership skills is also a critical success factor. As Dr. Robert Schuller has said, "If it is to be, it's up to me."

At the start of this book, you took the Superstar Leadership Test as a quick way to introduce you to the key management approaches. At this point, you should be ready for a more detailed assessment that should help you formulate an action plan. Go to our Website (*www.wcwpartners. com*) and click on Superstar Leadership Assessment. As you read the next section, keep an open mind and challenge yourself to reach new levels of performance effectiveness.

How Great Can You Be?

Scientists debate whether people use only 10 percent or less of their potential.[1] Others believe the potential of human intelligence is unlimited. For leaders, the bottom line is that people have incredible potential. Superstars leaders all of the strategies we have been discussing to help bring out the best in others. How great can you be as a manager? Do you buy into excuses such as the following?

▸ I don't have time.

▸ The company doesn't support me.

▸ It's tough out there.

▸ The employees don't have a work ethic anymore.

▸ We need new tools and technology.

▸ Customers don't understand.

▸ I tried.

▸ I can't.

The "whine list" can go on and on. Managers who make excuses forget what President Harry S. Truman said, "The buck stops here." As the manager, you are accountable and responsible. It is your responsibility to overcome the obstacles you meet.

Be Proactive, Not Reactive

Great achievements do not happen without good planning. We are built to think and to plan, and good managers put that attribute to regular use. Consider the Human Genome Project, an effort that identified the human DNA map cell-by-cell and essentially uncovered the mystery of life. DNA mapping literally changes the medical field from a reactive discipline to a proactive one. Some scientists predict that if a baby has a predisposition for disease before it is born, doctors could switch the cells to make them preventive. Ethical considerations aside, the fact remains that human intellect has discovered this incredible technology.

Although you most likely aren't a human genome scientist, this example demonstrates the huge potential of a person to identify and solve problems, and that is an important part of a manager's job. Managers think proactively and creatively, and then work to achieve their goals. Think, act, and believe—big, bigger, biggest.

Be Action-Oriented, Not Apathetic

Direct managers have the biggest influence on employee performance. These front-line managers have an incredible opportunity to make a difference, but too often they take this responsibility lightly. They give up, react negatively, or let events push them around; they focus on themselves instead.

A sports magazine recently reported on a man who ran 90 marathons in a year and claimed a place in the Guinness Book of World Records. In the year 2000, that man said he would run 200 marathons in honor of the new millennium—and he did. When asked why, he replied that he didn't want anyone to break his record, and he knew he could do it.

We asked managers in a leadership program if any of them had ever run a marathon. One company president said he did but that "one is enough."

It's not about running marathons. It's about the attitude that motivates the runner. Managers know that some days on the job feel like marathons, but managers using the right tools—goal-setting, training, coaching, problem-solving, communicating—can get through those marathon days with success. Superstar leaders tap into their employees' reservoirs of ability and stamina—as well as their own—and get the jobs done.

Think of the Potential, Not the Problems

Cliff Miedl was a 20-year-old plumber's apprentice. While working on a job, he accidentally drove his jackhammer through three high-voltage cables, sending 30,000 volts of electricity charging through his body (15 times more than a death sentence in an electric chair). The jolt blew off most of his toes, shattered his knees, exploded part of his skull, and put a hole in his back as the electricity left his body. His heart stopped beating three times, yet he survived. Doctors said he'd never walk again.

Yet, through a slow and painful recovery, he learned to walk again. Not only that, but he was inspired by the story of 1988 Olympian Greg Barton, who had clubfeet and won two gold medals in kayaking. Cliff learned to kayak and made the 2000 U.S. Olympic team. On opening night of the Sydney Games, the 603 members of the team voted him the flag bearer for their march into the stadium. Cliff turned a tragedy into triumph with an indomitable spirit. Though he didn't win a medal, he certainly is a superstar!

Employee performance problems can be difficult, but they are nothing compared to Cliff's ordeal. Superstar leaders manage the difficulties by focusing on what they can control, and they don't waste their time on things they can't control. The human spirit offers a magnificent potential for success.

Managers often work with less than the best talent, but they can turn average employees into champions.

In summary, never underestimate your or others' ability to excel and succeed. People want to do a good job. Almost all employees can make their performance significantly better; they just need guidance to get it done. That's your job.

How great can you be? How good do you want to be? The Superstar Leadership Model has given you the tools you need to achieve incredible results; if you are willing to use them consistently and passionately, you can achieve the next level. Do the next Superstar Leader Application as you anticipate success.

Day 29 Superstar Leader Application
Directions: Rate yourself on the following in terms of how often you engage in the listed behavior. Use a scale of 1 to 5, with 5 = very frequently and 1 = rarely.
☐ I understand and apply the concepts of employee motivation.
☐ I am aware of the High-Performance Formula.
☐ I set clear goals and expectations with employees.
☐ I manage employee performance proactively.
☐ I give helpful and constructive feedback to employees.
☐ I handle employees' performance problems appropriately.
☐ I listen well in one-on-one situations.
☐ I listen effectively within the organization.
☐ I communicate effectively by creating a positive communication climate.

☐ I treat all people respectfully.
☐ I use good rapport skills in interactions with others.
☐ I look to get outside the box and expand mental models when dealing with people and problems.
☐ I handle confrontation and conflict constructively.
☐ I view all employee interactions as coaching opportunities.
☐ I coach effectively in one-on-ones.
☐ I coach informally frequently.
☐ I give regular positive feedback or praise to employees.
☐ I reward employees effectively for higher performance.
☐ I understand and apply the principles of recognition.
☐ I deliver engaging and practical group training.
☐ I provide effective OJT to employees.
☐ I know employees well enough to manage them according to their needs.
☐ I manage with flexibility based on the needs of employees.
☐ I provide promotions and incentives as appropriate to challenge employees.
☐ I create a fun working environment.
☐ I have goals and plans to improve results.
☐ I look for ways to be innovative and continuously improve.
☐ I seek to consistently apply the Superstar leadership strategies.
List five or six of your leadership strengths.
List two or three of the areas in which you need to improve.
List your action steps for consistent execution.

Coaches who can outline plays on a black board are a dime a dozen. The ones who win get inside their player and motivate.

—Vince Lombardi

Day 30
EXECUTION EXCELLENCE

When you think of the word *superstar*, who comes to mind? Sports fans might think of Drew Brees, Jack Nicklaus, Wayne Gretsky, Michael Jordan, Ray Lewis, or Roger Clemens. Moviegoers might think of Meryl Streep, Harrison Ford, or Brad Pitt. Or maybe a musician such as Lady Gaga, Pavarotti, or Paul McCartney comes to mind. Someone might think of talk-show host Oprah Winfrey. The one person who probably didn't come to mind is you.

During one of our training sessions, we asked everyone to name a superstar, and the group shouted out the name of one of their customer service representatives, Scott. Though he wouldn't be a superstar in your eyes, he had become one in the eyes of his coworkers; he was a top achiever, and he did his job extremely well. You don't have to make the cover of *Time* magazine to be exceptional at what you do, nor do you have to be a celebrity to be a superstar or good boss.

All superstars have one thing in common: They are consistently good at what they do. You, too, can be consistently good and achieve superstar status on the job. Use effective strategies and be consistent, day in and day out. With deliberate practice and excellent execution, you and your employees will achieve better results.

Excellent execution requires thoughtful planning, scheduling, and careful review of the results. It also demands determination, discipline, and persistence. Look at the following graphic and rate yourself for clarity, competence, commitment, consistency, and execution, which is the combined total of the other ratings.

Driving Results

As shown in the Driving Results graphic, consistency can be defined in terms of three characteristics:

1. Clarity.
2. Competence.
3. Commitment.

These three characteristics are important for the execution of any plan. Clarity means understanding the goals—smart goals with well-outlined roles and action steps. Competence is the knowledge, skills, and information required for the task. Commitment is the desire to do whatever it takes to get the job done.

Study the ratings on the following graphic. The ratings for clarity, competence, and commitment are combined, and the total is divided by the consistency rating to obtain the execution rating—the likelihood of success. High clarity, competence, and commitment ratings coupled with a low number on the consistency rating result in a very good execution rating, which means your results will most likely be superior.

Consistency Creates Success

Rating Each of the 3 C's	Rating Consistency	Rating Interpretation
5 = To a very high degree	1 = Almost always	11–15 = High propensity for successful execution outcome
4 = To a high degree	2 = To a high degree	
3 = To some degree	3 = Occasionally	6–10 = Some success potential; Additional development needed
2 = To a small degree	4 = Seldom	
1 = To a very small degree	5 = Almost never	0–5 = Low/No chance of successful execution outcome

The following graphic demonstrates what occurs when consistency wavers.

Lack of Consistency Destroys Success

Rating Each of the 3 C's	Rating Consistency	Rating Interpretation
5 = To a very high degree	1 = Almost always	11–15 = High propensity for successful execution outcome
4 = To a high degree	2 = To a high degree	
3 = To some degree	3 = Occasionally	6–10 = Some success potential; Additional development needed
2 = To a small degree	4 = Seldom	
1 = To a very small degree	5 = Almost never	0–5 = Low/No chance of successful execution outcome

Notice that if consistency decreases even slightly, the overall execution rating is cut in half. This means your results will most likely be poor. Time after time, managers kick off new initiatives, only to fail in the ongoing implementation. Things start off well, but the consistency of application decreases bit by bit. Employees are skeptical of new initiatives because they know the follow-through will be weak based on many past experiences.

You need staying power to achieve extraordinary results using the Superstar Leadership Strategies. You have to be in it for the long term. You have to be persistent. Persistence, determination, and consistency separate the winners from the losers—Superstar leaders from bad bosses.

Greg is sensational. His results are about two-and-a half times the company average. He has helped his employees make a lot of money and enjoy the process. He is a good boss; we call him a Superstar. We asked him what he has learned. He responded with the following keys to his success:

- It's about the employees and how to make them successful.
- Communicate all the time.
- Always have something going on.
- Keep coaching.
- Recognize and reward consistently.
- Have clear goals and expectations.
- Have fun.

In Day 1, we asked three questions:

1. How effective is management today?
2. How does this affect employee satisfaction and engagement?
3. What do leaders need to do?

Let's review what leaders need to do.

What Do Leaders Need to Do?

▸ Clear goals and expectations: 16-percent improvement!
▸ Training: Companies in the top quarter of training expense ($1,500 per year or more) average 24-percent higher profit margins.
▸ Communication: 30-percent increase on market value!
▸ Coaching: 88-percent impact!
▸ Leadership flexibility: double the profits.
▸ Recognition: triple return on equity for companies with more recognition than those companies who do less.
▸ Promotions/incentives: 22-percent impact on results!
▸ Customer loyalty: 5-percent improvement in customer retention improves profit 25% or more!
▸ Hiring: The wrong hire costs three times the annual salary.

Our experiences as described often in this book and the research support the Superstar Leadership Model. Notice the chart as it illustrates our leadership model:

Superstar Leadership Model
How to Revolutionize Performance

If you do these strategies consistently and passionately, you will gain high performances from your people because you are doing it. You won't just be a good boss; you will become a Superstar leader. How do you know if you have achieved this? You are a Superstar leader when you consistently achieve exceptional results while still improving and your team enjoys the process.

Notice the orbital effect of the Superstar Leadership Model. Think about how the planets rotate around the sun, consistently and without chaos, keeping the planet Earth safe. Superstar leaders are able to keep things in line. Why? Because their people become independent, self-directed performers because of the Superstar leader's efforts. Bad bosses manage in chaos; their companies and departments are scattered and disjointed, and it's amazing anything of value gets done.

The Superstar Leadership Strategies are interrelated. Communication and recognition are linked together. Training, coaching, and focusing on goals all go hand-in-hand as bosses strive for continuous improvement in service and quality. Incentives provide motivation and add an element of fun to the workplace. Consistency ties the strategies together as teams work together and achieve higher levels of success.

The great violinist Paganini was approached by an admirer who said, "I would give half my life to play like you."

Paganini replied, "I did give up half my life."

You don't have to give up your life to be a Superstar, but the life you put into your work can be more satisfying and successful if you consistently apply the strategies.

Day 30 Superstar Leader Application
Think of a time when you did your best work.
What were the elements of your success?
How many of the Superstar Leadership Strategies did you apply?
What can you do to stick with it and be consistent?

What the mind of man can conceive and believe, he can achieve.
—William Clement Stone

Day 31
IN SUMMARY:
THE SUPERSTAR LEADERSHIP PRESENCE

How do you get someone to follow you? Successful leaders have found that it isn't position power that matters most in the employee/ supervisory relationship. Personal power is the real key. Leaders take people to where they want to go. Great leaders take people to where they ought to be. That's the essence of the Superstar leader's presence.

Leadership through position power involves these strategies:

▸ Dictatorial approach.

▸ Employees are subordinate.

▸ "Do as I say!"

▸ Fear strategies.

▸ The leader has all the answers.

▸ Self-focus; seeking personal victory.

Leadership through personal power includes these strategies:

▸ Engagement approach.

▸ Employees are partners.

▸ "Do as I do also!"

▸ Lead by example.

▸ Influencing strategies.

▸ The team has the answers, too.

▸ Others focus; caring enough to help others win.

This is an exciting time to be a leader. Never before has there been so much statistical evidence linked to leadership effectiveness. True leadership effectiveness has more to do with who you are and less to do with your job title.

What Are the Characteristics of Leadership?

We believe Superstar leaders embody two main characteristics: integrity and caring. Integrity involves living a life that is genuine and honest.

It's an internal value about how to interact with the world. Caring is about treating all people with dignity. Superstar leaders truly focus on helping other people become successful as a way to their success.

Other work supports this thinking. Through research in the 1980s and again in the 1990s, Jim Kouzes and Barry Posner found four crucial characteristics from an exhaustive list of more than 225 different values, traits, and characteristics. Their methodology included a questionnaire and later case studies. The following open-ended question summarized the views of more than 20,000 managers from four continents: What values (personal traits or characteristics) do you look for and admire in your superiors?[1]

What they found is that people want to follow leaders who are honest, forward-looking, inspiring, and competent. Following is our definition of each of these characteristics.

Being Honest

Be ethical, tell the truth, and do what you say you will do. Considering all of the celebrity types across industries and vocations that have bit the dust, this is not surprising and even more crucial today. Honesty, integrity, and ethics are in great demand! More and more companies have created ethical statements as guidelines for behavior in the business. Doing business the right way is becoming more crucial than being the best. After all, if you are dishonest, it affects the trust you have in your relationships with employees and customers alike, and it erodes the foundation of your inner conscience. It's been stated, "To thine own self be true." If you aren't, how can you be with others or really achieve success as a leader?

In his book *Principled-Centered Leadership*, Stephen Covey defines integrity as: "Honestly matching words and feelings with thoughts and actions, with no desire other than for the good of others, without malice or desire to deceive, take advantage, manipulate, or control, constantly reviewing your intent as you strive for congruence."[2] How do you know if you are acting with integrity? Here are some indicators:

▸ You keep your word.

▸ You follow up on your commitments.

▸ Your behavior and values match.

▸ In spite of your mood, you treat people respectfully.

▸ You don't need to drop names, situations, or events in conversations to impress people.

▸ You strive to do the right thing not the expedient thing.

▶ When under temptation to bend the rules, you stay honorable to the company's values and what's right.

▶ You treat all people with respect and dignity.

▶ Poor taste in humor is not part of your vocabulary.

▶ Cynicism and sarcasm are not useful to you.

▶ You are a good listener, even if another's views are different from your own.

Being Forward-Looking

Have a vision for the future, and clearly communicate it. Yes, focus on the short term, but have a plan for tomorrow. Leaders need to hold both of these simultaneously in their hands.

Being Inspiring

Have some passion and enthusiasm for what you do; it's contagious. If you can't get genuinely excited about what you are doing, it's almost impossible to get others to be.

Being Competent

Be a student of the game, and keep learning about your business and how to deal with people. Stephen Covey's seven habits also relate to the fact that an effective person is more apt to be an effective leader. His seven habits are:[3]

1. **Be proactive.** Change begins from within; make the decision to improve your life.

2. **Begin with the end in mind.** Have a personal mission statement with long-term goals.

3. **Put first things first.** Focus on the key roles and priorities in your life.

4. **Think win/win.** Seek relationships and agreements that are mutually beneficial.

5. **Seek first to understand, then to be understood.** Be an effective listener; it's the bedrock of trusting relationships.

6. **Synergize.** Communicate with mutual trust and understanding.

7. **Sharpen the saw.** Keep learning and maintain a balance in life to renew your effectiveness.

Being a Superstar Leader

Famed plastic surgeon Dr. Maxwell Maltz discovered that things on the outside don't make the person on the inside. After many surgeries to remake the appearance of his patients, he found most still struggled with low self-concepts. One in particular had a crooked nose fixed, so she looked similar to Greta Garbo. Yet the patient told Dr. Maltz that she still felt ugly.[4]

Success is indeed a state of mind; it has to do with the self-image. In fact, Emerson said, "Self-esteem is the first step to success." Leading is a state of mind, a habit that can be cultivated. Certainly, obstacles will arise. The farmer faces hazardous weather, insects, and market deviations. The successful farmer is persistent day in and day out, year in and year out. Leaders take the same approach whatever the problems are.

How Do Superstar Leaders Succeed?

Leaders go within. What counts most is their mental attitude and image. Leaders imagine the best, not the worst. They think about what they want, not what they don't want. Then they act. Leaders pre-play positive outcomes and don't replay negative situations. Leaders create the futures they image and don't lament past mistakes or lost opportunities.

Dick Fosbury, inventor of the Fosbury Flop, used imaging to set a world record in the high jump of 7' 3". He also won the gold medal in the 1968 Olympics. He'd rock back and forth a few times at the starting line to simulate his run and jump. Then he'd take off, run, and high jump backward over the bar. He was a world champion—a leader and innovator in his field.

Others have used positive imaging, too. Jean Claude Killy won three Olympic gold medals using this technique. Golf champions over time—Tom Watson, Gary Player, Jack Nicklaus, and Tiger Woods—visualized each shot before they took it. Why? Because it helps them refocus on their best form, not on the errors.

Some of the most exceptional examples of successful positive imaging are astronauts. Nobody knew what the *Apollo* moon expeditions would really be like, except maybe Jules Verne or Ray Bradbury. However, the astronauts performed their tasks with precision. Thousands of hours of review and practice in the desert and ocean made them winners. They pre-played the end result with NASA simulations.

Neil Armstrong said of the moon expedition, "It was beautiful, just like the drill."

Pete Conrad concurred: "It feels like I've been there many times before."

How Does This Apply to You?

No matter what your job, you can improve the results. Superstar leaders make the attempt; losers quit. Superstar leaders view what they do as a challenge. They look ahead and look within to bring out their best. They don't settle for mediocrity in sales, technical competence, expertise, knowledge, people skills, or management ability. Losers complain, stick with the status quo, and never get involved to make things better.

Do you face obstacles? Sure! But so did the POWs in Vietnam. Many spent three to seven years behind bars, deprived of most intellectual activity or physical comforts. To combat boredom and loneliness, they took self-development courses in their minds. Some learned to play the guitar and piano without even touching the instrument. They used make-believe instruments made of sticks. Colonel George Hall maintained his golf skills by playing 18 holes of golf in his mind every day.

Do you want to be a good boss—maybe a Superstar leader? Start by continuing your personal development. Focus on the outcomes, not the obstacles. If you fail, ask: "What can I learn from this, and what will I do better or differently next time?" Then remember the people you work with—your team. You are either part of the solution or you're an ally to the problem. Scientist Albert Einstein was asked what advice he had for the schools. He suggested that the student be allowed to think for one hour a day to figure out for themselves all the ideas and theories they are taught. This is good advice for leaders as well. This internalization process is part of really knowing yourself. Think about how you are thinking.

Leadership is a science and an art. It's a science because it has been studied, and specific management practices and skills achieve better results than others. Managers can learn these, like we have been doing throughout *Superstar Leadership*. It's an art because there are two main variables in using the practices: the thought patterns and values of individual managers and their degree of application of the practices and skills. As we have stated, effective leaders become more effective if they have a keen awareness of what they can or cannot do, and what they will and will not do.

Know thyself as the philosopher, Socrates advised. It helps you know where you really are starting from—a launching pad to higher performance.

You need to take a personal inventory. This book has helped you do that and helped you learn and apply ways to build up your strengths and to minimize your weaknesses. You also need to look at your beliefs and values about yourself and the world you live in. We discussed this when we reviewed our mental models. Yet to succeed, you need to focus your beliefs, attributes, and skills to the job at hand and to do it with great purpose and intention. At age 17, Terry Fox learned he had cancer in his leg. A few days after his 18th birthday, it was amputated. The night before the operation, Terry dreamed he was running across Canada.

Soon, Terry was fitted with an artificial limb. He began to run across Canada with a purpose in mind: to help eliminate or get rid of cancer. He set a goal to raise $1 million for the Canadian Cancer Society. After running three-fifths of the way, the cancer spread, and Terry soon died. He didn't complete his run, yet he raised 1.7 million dollars for the Canadian Cancer Society, and he positively touched the lives of thousands of people through his courage and purpose. Through his foundation, millions more have been raised, and the lives of millions have been touched. The Terry Fox Foundation announced on April 12, 2010, that its total fundraising efforts for cancer research had reached the $500 million mark.

All people need purpose or, as self-help author Napoleon Hill declared, "A definite chief aim" for their lives.[5] Leaders do, too! A purpose is bigger than a goal. All goals sprout from your purpose. A goal has a beginning, middle, and end. Purposes aren't always that easily defined. Yet to be effective, they must be simply stated. A purpose is a lighthouse to the goal-ships in your life. Companies have vision and mission statements, and people have purpose statements.

What is your purpose? You may or may not really know. For now, just get an idea of what you think it is. By identifying a purpose, you tie all of your efforts together. You will also be able to stay on track during the good times as well as the bad. A purpose answers the question "What difference does it make, really?" It provides you clear focus. We have learned that Superstar leaders tie their successes to the process of helping their people succeed.

What is success, after all? Money, bank accounts, the stock market, Internet savvy, or a PhD? An article in a major newspaper a few years back gave some clues. It described two people. The first was a lobbyist who made a large, six-figure income. He lived in the most expensive Washington, D.C., neighborhood and related to the highest government officials.

He said his life had no meaning. The other person was a single parent who finished high school taking night classes. She also worked, making $13,000 a year. She was excited and declared that life was full of possibilities.

Successful leaders are self-assured. They know their purpose, strengths, weaknesses, and what their good at.

Superstar leaders act with powerful intentions using the nine strategies reviewed in this book and maintaining utmost personal integrity in and during the process. This book has helped you do that and helped you learn and apply ways to build up your strengths and to minimize your weaknesses. We wish you the best of success.

We have this dream that soars on golden wings,

We visualize your achievements and your legacy
that sings.

We do not know all about your awesome goals or
your persistent efforts to raise the bar,

We only know that you are the best—a Superstar!

NOTES

Day 1

1. Amy Zipkin, "The Wisdom of Thoughtfulness" (*The New York Times,* May 31, 2000), p. C1.
2. "The Cost of Incivility" (*Time,* February 7, 2005).
3. Conference Board Report (January 2010).
4. "Getting Personal in the Workplace" (*Gallup Management Journal,* June 10, 2005).
5. "Giving Employees What They Want: The Returns Are Huge" (*Knowledge@Wharton,* May 4, 2005).
6. J. Hogan, R. Hogan, and R.B. Kaiser, "Management Derailment: Personality Assessment and Mitigation." In S. Zedeck (Ed.), *American Psychological Association Handbook of Industrial and Organizational Psychology* (Washington, D.C.: American Psychological Association, 2009).
7. M.R. Yessian, "Toward Effective Human Services Management" (*Public Administration Quarterly,* Spring 1988, 12, 1), p. 115.
8. Ken Blanchard, with Patricia Zigarmi and Drea Zigarmi, *Leadership and the One Minute Manager: Increasing Effectiveness Through Situational Leadership* (HarperCollins Business, 1985).
9. Hogan, Hogan, and Kaiser, pp. 4–5.
10. "What Managers Don't Know" (*Communication Briefings, Volume 8, Number 2,* 1990).
11. Ibid.
12. Ibid.
13. Ibid.
14. Ibid.
15. Ibid.
16. Mary Walton, *The Deming Management Method* (Penguin Group, 1986), pp. 138–139.
17. Roger Hale and Rita Maehling, *Recognition Redefined* (Tenant Company, 1992), p. 18.
18. "What Managers Don't Know."
19. Michael LeBeouf, *The Greatest Management Principle in the World* (Putnam and Sons, 1985), p. 20.
20. "US Job Satisfaction Lowest in Two Decades" (Conference Board, June 2010).
21. Tom Rath, *65% of Americans Receive No Praise or Recognition in the Workplace* (Gallup Organization's bucketbook.com, August 2004).
22. Steve Crabtree, "Getting Personal in the Workplace" (*Gallup Management Journal, 2004: The Carnegie Management Group, The Disengagement Crisis,* 2010).
23. Dody Tsiantar, "The Cost of Incivility" (*Time,* Biz Briefs, February 7, 2005).
24. Andrea Davis, "*Employee Disengagement: What Should Employers Expect in 2010?*" (Articlesbase Website, *www.articlesbase.com,* November 2009).
25. Onyx Global HR, "The Power of Recognition: Retaining Your Talent" (Articlesbase Website, *www.articlesbase.com,* May 2010).

26. Edwin Locke and Gary Latham, *Goalsetting: A Motivational Technique That Works!* (Prentice Hall, 1984), pp. 16–17.
27. Susan J. Wells, "Value of Training" (*HR Magazine,* April 2001).
28. "Effective Communication Liked to Greater Shareholder Value" (Watson Wyatt Study, 2002).
29. G. Olivero, K.D. Bane, and R.E. Kopelman, "Executive Coaching as a Transfer of Training Tool: Effects on Productivity in a Public Agency" (*Public Personnel Management,* Winter 1997, 26, 4), pp. 461–469.
30. Jack Zenger, Joe Folkman, and Scott Edinger, "How Extraordinary Leaders Double Profits" (Chief Learning Officer, 2009).
31. Adrian Gostick and Chester Elton, *The Carrot Principle: How the Best Managers Use Recognition to Engage Their Employees, Retain Talent, and Drive Performance* (Free Press, 2007), p. 17.
32. "Scientific Studies Highlighting the Benefits of Tangible Rewards over Cash" (IncentiveProgram.com, March 2008).
33. Fred Reicheld, *The Ultimate Question* (Harvard Business School Press, 2006), p.15.
34. "Hiring the Wrong Person Costs You 3X Their Annual Salary" (Personnel Policy Service, Inc., 2010).

Day 2

1. Frederick Herzberg, "One More Time: How Do You Motivate Employees?" (*Harvard Business Review,* September–October 1987).
2. "Linking Employee Satisfaction with Productivity, Performance and Customer Satisfaction" (Corporate Leadership Council, July 2003), Corporate Executive Board Catalogue Number: CLC114T2FJ.
3. Alex Edmans, "Does the Stock Market Fully Value Intangibles? Employee Satisfaction and Equity Prices" (University of Pennsylvania, The Wharton School, June 2010).

Day 3

1. Jad Mouawad, "Pushing 40, Southwest Is Still Playing the Rebel" (*New York Times,* November 20, 2010).
2. Crystal Arcand, "Seven Warning Signs of a Bad Boss" (Associated Content, March 2007).

Day 6

1. Gary R. McClain and Deborah S. Romaine, *The Everything Managing People Book: Quick and Easy Ways to Build, Motivate, and Nurture a First-Rate Team, 2nd Edition* (Everything Books, 2007).

Day 7

1. Abraham Maslow, "A Theory of Human Motivation" (*Psychological Review,* 1943, 50, 4), pp. 370–396.
2. Robert Conklin, *How to Get People to Do Things* (Mass Market Paperback, 1985).

Day 8

1. John Baldoni, "Powerful Leadership Communication (*Leader to Leader,* 2004), pp. 20–24.
2. Tom Peters, *Liberation Management* (New York: Alfred A. Knopf, 1992).
3. Dr. Albert Mehrabian, *Silent Messages: Implicit Communication of Emotions and Attitudes* (Belmont, Calif.: Wadsworth, 1981; currently distributed by Albert Mehrabian, [am@ kaaj.com]).

4. Daniel Goleman, *Emotional Intelligence* (New York: Bantam Books, 1995).
5. Tom Peters and Bob Waterman, *In Search of Excellence* (New York: Grand Central Publishing, 1982).
6. Ronn Torossian, "The 5 Biggest Crisis PR Blunders of 2011" (*Business Insider,* December 7, 2011).

Day 9
1. Peter Senge, *The Fifth Discipline* (Doubleday/Currency, 1990).
2. Steven Covey, *The 7 Habits of Highly Effective People* (New York: Free Press, 1989).

Day 11
1. Peters and Waterman, *In Search of Excellence..*
2. Covey, *The 7 Habits.*

Day 12
1. Olivero, Bane, and Kopelman, "Executive Coaching as a Transfer of Training Tool," p. 461.

Day 13
1. Pat Riley, *The Winner Within* (New York: The Berkeley Publishing Group, 1993).

Day 14
1. Roger Hale and Rita Maehling, *Recognition Redefined* (Tenant Company, 1992), p. 18.
2. Marcus Buckingham and Curt Coffman, *First, Break All the Rules* (New York: Simon and Schuster, 1999).
3. Ken Blanchard, *The One Minute Manage*r (New York: William Morrow and Company, 1982).
4. Bob Nelson, *1001 Ways to Recognize Employees* (New York: Workman Publishing, 1994).

Day 16
1. Adrian Gostick and Chester Elton, *The Carrot Principle* (New York: Free Press, 2007), p. 11.

Day 17
1. Leigh Branham, *The 7 Hidden Reasons Employees Leave: How to Recognize the Subtle Signs and Act Before It's Too Late* (Amacom, 2005).
2. Caroll Lachnit, *Training Magazine,* September 2001. Cited in Branham, *The 7 Hidden Reasons Employees Leave.*
3. Geoff Colvin, *Talent Is Overrated* (New York: The Penguin Group, 2008).

Day 18
1. James Kouzes and Barry Posner, *The Leadership Challenge* (New York: John Wiley and Sons, 2002).

Day 19
1. John Jones, William Bearley, Doug Watsabaugh, *The New Fieldbook for Trainers* (Amherst, Mass.: HRD Press, 1996).

Day 20
1. Daniel Goleman, *Primal Leadership* (Harvard Business School Publishing, 2002).

Day 21
1. Paul Hersey and Kenneth H. Blanchard, *Management and Organizational Behavior* (Englewood Cliffs, N.J.: Prentice-Hall, 1988); Paul Hersey, *The Situational Leader* (Escondido, Calif.: Center for Leadership Studies, 1984). For an interview with Paul Hersey on the origins of the model, see John R.

Schermerhorn, Jr., "Situational Leadership: Conversations with Paul Hersey" (*Mid-American Journal of Business,* Fall 1997), pp. 5–12. Also see Claude L. Graeff, "The Situational Leadership Theory: A Critical View" (*Academy of Management Review,* Vol. 8, 1983), pp. 285–291, and the research summary in Gary Yukl, *Leadership in Organizations, Sixth Edition* (Upper Saddle River, N.J.: Pearson, 2006), pp. 223–225.

Day 24
1. Valarie Zeithaml, A. Parasuraman, and Dr. Leonard Berry, *Delivering Quality Service* (New York: The Free Press, 1990).

Day 25
1. William Oncken, *Managing Management Time: Get Them Monkeys off Your Back* (New York: Prentice Hall, 1987).

Day 27
1. Amy Chulik, "Employers Reveal Candidates' Most Unusual Job Interview Behavior," (The Hiring Site Powered by Career Builder Website, *thehiringsite. careerbuilder.com/2010/02/24/ employers-reveal-candidates-most-unusual-job-interview-behavior/,* February 24, 2010).

Day 29
1. The "10 percent" statistic has been cited in many sources, among them "Ten Percent and Counting" from BrainConnection.com (*www.brainconnection.com/ topics/?main=fa/brain-myth*), "The Ten-Percent Myth" from the *Skeptical Inquirer* (*www.csicop.org/ si/9903/ten-percent-myth.html*), "The Ten-Percent Myth" from Snopes. com (*www.snopes.com/science/ stats/10percnt.htm*), K.L. Higbee and S.L. Clay, "College Students' Beliefs in the Ten-Percent Myth" from *Journal of Psychology* (132:469–476, 1998), and B.L. Beyerstein, "Whence Cometh the Myth that We Only Use 10% of Our Brains?" in *Mind Myths: Exploring Popular Assumptions about the Mind and Brain* (edited by S. Della Sala, Chichester: John Wiley & Sons, pp. 3–24, 1999).

Day 31
1. Kouzes and Posner, *The Leadership Challenge.*
2. Stephen R. Covey, *Principle-Centered Leadership* (New York: Simon and Schuster, New York, 1990.
3. Covey, *The 7 Habits.*
4. Maxwell Maltz, *Psycho-Cybernetics* (New York: Pocket Books, 1960).
5. Napoleon Hill, *Think and Grow Rich* (New York: Fawcett Crest, 1960).

INDEX

ABOUT THE
AUTHORS

Rick Conlow

There aren't many who'd argue the fact that Rick is one enthusiastic guy. Even the titles of his training programs reflect his drive and positive energy.

A quick glance at his professional resume leaves you with the strong impression that effort and optimism are a winning combination. Case in point: With Rick by their side, clients have achieved double- and triple-digit improvement in their sales performance, quality, customer loyalty, and service results over the past 20-plus years, and earned more than 30 quality and service awards.

In a day and age where optimism and going the extra mile can sound trite, Rick has made them a differentiator. His clients include organizations that are leaders in their industries, as well as others that are less recognizable. Regardless, their goals are his goals.

Rick's life view and extensive background in sales and leadership—as a general manager, vice president, training director, program director, national sales trainer, and consultant—are the foundation of his coaching, training, and consulting services. Participants in Rick's experiential, live-action programs walk away with a-has, inspiration, and skills they can immediately put to use.

These programs include BEST Selling!, Moments of Magic!, Excellence in Management!, SuperSTAR Service and Selling!, The Greatest Secrets of all Time!, and SuperSTAR Leadership! Rick has also authored *Excellence in Management, Excellence in Supervision, Returning to Learning,* and *Moments of Magic.* He and his business partner, Doug Watsabaugh, recently published six new books, including *SuperSTAR Customer Service.*

When he's not engaging an audience or engrossed in a coaching discussion, this proud husband and father is most likely astride a weight bench or motorcycle, taking on the back roads and highways of Minnesota.

Doug Watsabaugh

Doug values being a "regular person," with his feet on the ground and head in the realities of the daily challenges his clients face. His heart for and experience in helping clients deal with difficult situations distinguish him from other sales performance and leadership development consultants.

His knowledge of experiential learning, and his skill at designing change processes and learning events have enabled him to measurably improve the lives of thousands of individuals and hundreds of organizations in a wide variety of industries (financial services, manufacturing, medical devices, consumer goods, and technology, to name a few).

Before starting his own business, Doug served as the director of operations for a national training institute, manager of organization development for a major chemical company, and was responsible for worldwide training and organization development for the world's third largest toy company.

He was also a partner in Performance & Human Development LLC, a California company that published high-involvement experiential activities, surveys and instruments, interactive training modules, papers, and multimedia presentations.

Doug has co-authored two books with John E. Jones, PhD, and William L. Bearley, Ed D: *The New Fieldbook for Trainers* (published by HRD Press and Lakewood Publishing) and *The OUS Quality Item Pool*, about organizational survey items that measure Baldrige criteria.

He is a member of the American Society for Training and Development (ASTD), the Minnesota Quality Council, and the National Organization Development Network.

Doug's father taught him the value of hard work, and it paid dividends. He funded his college education playing guitar and singing with a rock-n-roll band, experiencing a close call with fame when he played bass in concert with Chuck Berry (not bad for a guy who admits to being "a bit shy").

Although Doug's guitar remains a source of enjoyment, it pales in comparison to his number-one joy and priority: his family.

ABOUT
WCW PARTNERS, INC.

WCW Partners is a performance-improvement company focused on improving top line, sales, customer loyalty, and profits. We use nine key performance drivers to evaluate and help a company more quickly increase results and sustain them.

Based in Minneapolis/St. Paul, Minnesota, we work with clients in a variety of industries worldwide to help them excel in sales, service, and market leadership. We facilitate business growth and vitality through four practices—sales and customer retention improvement, organization and leadership development, innovation, and communications strategy.

Who We Are

We don't mind telling you that we're different than most consulting firms you'll find in the marketplace. For one thing, it's our approach. When you hire us, you get us. But just as important, we're people who've had to wrestle with the same issues you have: how to strengthen sales, boost productivity, improve quality, increase employee satisfaction, build a team, or retain and attract new customers. To us, "We develop the capability in you" is more than a catchy phrase. It's our promise.

Our Experience

Our clients include 3M, American Express, American Medical Systems, Amgen Inc., Accenture, AmeriPride Services, Andersen Windows, Avanade, Beltone, Canadian Linen and Uniform Service, Carew International, Case Corporation, Citigroup, Coca-Cola, Costco, Covance, Deknatel, Eaton Corporation, Electrochemicals Inc., Entergy, Esoterix, GeneralMills, GN Resound, GrantThornton, Hasbro Inc., Honeywell, Interton, Kenner Products, Marketlink, Kemps-Marigold, Meijer Corporation, National Computer Systems, Parker Brothers, Toro, Productive Workplace Systems, Red Wing Shoes, Rite Aid, Rollerblade, Ryan Companies, Schwan's Home Delivery, Target, Travelers Insurance, Thrivent, Tonka Corporation, and a number of nonprofit and educational institutions.

Contact Us

To learn how you can do amazing things, visit us on-line for additional materials and resources that can help your development and that of your team at *www.wcwpartners.com*, or contact Doug or Rick toll free at (888) 313–0514.